LOST *in* CYBERSPACE

LOST *in* CYBERSPACE

Essays and Far Fetched
T A L E S

Val Schaffner

Bridge Works Publishing Co.
Bridgehampton, New York

Copyright © 1993 Val Schaffner

All rights reserved under International Pan-American
Copyright Conventions. Published in the United States
by Bridge Works Publishing Co., Bridgehampton, New York.
Distributed in the U.S. by National Book Network, Lanham, Md.

Printed in the United States of America.
1   2   3   4   5   6   7   8   9   10
First Edition

Library of Congress Cataloging-in-Publication Data

Schaffner, Val.
Lost in cyberspace : essays and far-fetched tales / Val Schaffner.
           p.   cm.
          ISBN 1-882593-03-0 (hard : alk. paper)
                      I. Title.
PS3569.C46L6   1993   93-22636
    814′.54—dc20   CIP

Most of these essays appeared originally in a
somewhat different form in the *East Hampton* (*N.Y.*) *Star.*

Book and jacket design by Edith Allard

Printed in the United States of America

to Min-Myn

Contents

FOREWORD

By Bill Henderson   viii

C:\LUCIFER>

The Ghost in the Screen   3
Manuscripts Don't Burn   14
Virus Zero   19
Satan's Cellar   24

TWILIGHT OF THE GLUTTONS

Government Time   29
The Turkey   32
Gingerbread Man   36
The Lobster Trees   39
The Apple   44
The Mushroom   47

THE DEVIL AT THE WHEEL

Faust on the Freeway   53
Driving Lessons   56
Secret City   59
Virtual City   63
Dallas   66
No Smoking in the Parthenon   72
Hey Mr. Rockefeller   76

Contents

RIDING THE BOMB

The Lemon That Exploded 81

Atomic Fireballs 86

Gladiators and Astronauts 92

A Dream of Pluto 95

The Blue Crystal 99

1-800-LUCIFER 103

The Airplane of Youth 106

THE BEAST IN THE TREES

The Sachems 111

Chief Salamander 116

Cloud of Husbands 120

Nymphs in Light 123

The Grass Is Screaming 125

The Torrents of Sex 129

THE COUNTERFEITER

Art versus Art 135

Ah, Valpolicella! 140

The Impostor 144

The Noble Pretender 147

THE NIXOMAT

Nixon the Party Animal 153

Silver Fox 155

The Head 159

The Tantrum Alarm 164

LOST IN CYBERSPACE

Computer Lawyers 171

Virtual Delights 175

The Cursor 179

Foreword

by

Bill Henderson

—Publisher of The Pushcart Press,
originator of The Pushcart Press Prizes: Best of the Small Presses

I have known Val Schaffner for many years.

At first I knew him as this tall, silent fellow at the Wainscott, N.Y., Post Office. I nodded hello as I picked up my mail at a box near his and he nodded back. We did a lot of nodding.

Then I read his first essay in *The East Hampton Star*, our esteemed weekly paper, and I suddenly realized I had been nodding at an extraordinary guy. Each issue of the *Star* is boiling over with opinion, some written by the staff, most in letters to the editor—an amazing sound and fury stew. Helen Rattray, the *Star*'s editor, will print just about any letter that crosses her desk, presiding over a raucous New England town meeting in print. And she discovered Val Schaffner, and she gives his weekly column "Periscope" top billing. Schaffner even has his own boxed space on the editorial page.

And such a box! There Schaffner is frequently taking chances, usually making sense, often hilarious, and invariably new. Plus the man's whimsy is astounding. There's nothing like it anywhere.

Most introductions to gatherings such as this move through the book's contents and pick out favorites. But how to do this with so many favorites? The fact is that you can dip into Schaffner's collection just about any place and be rewarded amply. And informed too, with wacky facts.

Did you realize for instance that Ronald Reagan had his street number in Bel Air changed from 666 to 668 because 666 is the number of The Beast in The Book of Revelations? You will learn this and much more in "Secret City."

Have you been informed that some highly civilized people eat live octopus? (See "The Lobster Trees.")

Did you know that bears dine mostly on moths and when not eating moths they delight in mugging hikers by scaring them into dropping their picnic baskets? ("The Turkey")

Want to experience what it's like to be mugged in Dallas? Schaffner was. ("Dallas")

When you aren't learning these and hundreds of other curious details, Val Schaffner will keep you laughing too with his blend of musing and invention. He might even make you rich.

For instance "The Tantrum Alarm" suggests several inventions that could earn you a fortune. The Nixo-mat is a device that would allow you to secretly tape your party guests and replay the repartee the next day. The Writer's Seatbelt would belt writers into their desk chairs and not let them loose until they have written a pre-set number of pages.

And speaking of inventions, Val Schaffner has a pretty good idea who invented that infernal conspiracy that plunges us into early darkness every fall—Daylight Saving Time. He suspects light bulb manufacturers, oil producers, and astronomers. ("Government Time")

And when you have cleared up that little mystery, try following Schaffner's inspired logic about the origin of males singing in the shower. Something about peeper frogs mating in the spring and cave men washing off after a winter underground. ("The Torrents of Sex")

Even a topic as deadly serious as the Shoreham, N.Y., nuclear power plant can turn funny in Schaffner's word processor. He once owned a lemon—a Porsche—and the Long Island Lighting Company had a dud, too—the Shoreham plant. Find out what they have in common in "The Lemon That Exploded."

Equally memorable and chilling is Schaffner's piece "Atomic Fireballs"—one of the best recollections of the Cuban Missile Crisis I have ever read. Period.

I could go on and on, because each selection here is worth the price of admission. But Schaffner's task is not just to entertain. As the essays progress, a theme becomes apparent—his concern that one day there will be no more real travel, or real encounters with real angels and real villains. Instead, reality will become "virtual," and the humanist's humor, intellect and imagination will disappear into that nether world of high tech, cyberspace.

If I write any more, I will steal your joy. So read on, reader. Welcome to the mind and wit of Val Schaffner. There isn't an exploding lemon in the lot.

The Ghost
in the
Screen

Around the time I began to write on a computer, I became obsessed with a haunted house. I had made it so in a story about the ghosts that resided there, ghosts who liked to meet on the roof of its tower, which commands a fine view of Sag Harbor, N.Y., the old port town not far from where I live.

Ghosts, I assumed, are all around us every night—flocking together, observing us, making critical remarks that we cannot hear, and devising secret, undetected ways of influencing our actions to suit their purposes. I wrote the story from the point of view of some ghosts who declare an emergency because their haunted house is threatened by the wrecker's ball.

It was natural to locate them in this particular house, whose countenance was in fact ancient and powerfully foreboding. I often drove by it in the evening. It appeared deserted, though occasionally a light would glimmer in a tower window. Some of the windows were broken, the shingles were falling off, the yard was overgrown, and right next door was a cemetery.

The cemetery was full of sailors. Sag Harbor had been a prosperous whaling port, full of mansions erected with the profits from whale oil, until in the 1840s the depletion of the whales and the discovery of petroleum combined to throw the whalers out of work, whereupon many of them went to California to join the Gold Rush. Today it is known as the "un-Hampton"—a quieter, more authentic community than the other resort towns on Long Island's South Fork, the so-called Hamptons, where the character of the country villages they once were has been eclipsed by an idea that their summer residents bring with them from their city, a glossy fantasy of what country life ought to be, a counterfeit arcadia. For old ghosts, Sag Harbor is the last refuge.

In its cemetery there is a sculpture of a broken mast, a memorial to shipwreck victims. Another stone bears only these words: THOUGHTS ARE THINGS. That was the motto of the man who lies there, a local philosopher who moved to California with the gold miners but came home to die.

I don't know where the man who built the haunted house is buried, but his portrait hangs in the Whaling Museum, which also contains an orrery that he built: a clockwork model of the solar system. He was an astronomer, as was my great-grandfather; he was also a clock maker, and in the 1850s he designed a house for himself, including a wing for his huge library and an Italianate tower for his telescopes and pendulums. Perhaps he was a friend of the philosopher-miner who said, "Thoughts are things." Then their ghosts could be identified together on the roof of the tower, studying the rings of Saturn and disputing the nature of reality.

I had the beginning of an idea for another story. The narrator buys the astronomer's house. He is a writer, and he makes the tower room his office. On his desk is a computer. One night he forgets to switch it off. In the morning he finds a strange diagram on the screen: something like a series of concentric circles tagged with occult formulas. Worried, he runs an antivirus program. He leaves the computer on again to see if the phenomenon will recur. It does. There is a message: "Thoughts are things." Curious now, he leaves the machine running every night. And every morning when he sits down to work, there is something new on the screen: a list of celestial bodies, a horoscope, a woman's name (a name he finds on one of the stones in the cemetery), some map coordinates, an inventory of gold ingots, other messages in the form of obscure warnings.

The messages become longer, more specific, more disturbing. Whatever writes them now begins to load whole programs. They are games, apparently; some kind of virtual reality. There is one in particular that he does not care to play. Its command file is HELL.EXE.

If we don't yet associate computers with ghosts, that is because they haven't been with us long enough. A ghost might well choose to haunt one. Especially a ghost who was a scientist and clock maker, or a philosopher and writer. Or the Devil. An ethereal spirit could more easily manipulate the magnetic bits on my hard disk than more durable objects such as the keys of my old Underwood. Writing, anyway, has become a ghostlier act since the advent of the word processor. The words glimmer on the screen in a phantom limbo state. They are like spirits awaiting the printer's incarnation. (And why is this winking dash called the cursor? Whom does it curse?)

Around the time I was pondering the idea of the haunted computer, trying to figure out how to make it a story (titled "The Cursor"), I happened to drive by the astronomer's house and see a For Sale sign newly planted on the tangled lawn, with a phone number. I called the number and made an appointment with a real estate lady. Inside, the house was even more decrepit than it looked from the street. The walls were bursting with rot. Yet I imagined it to be pervaded with the original character of its builder the astronomer. And I had already fantasized about living there.

It turned out to be inhabited by two disheveled crones, who sat at the kitchen table without saying a word, each with a deck of cards, playing solitaire. According to the broker, they were mother and daughter, and they spent most of each day playing solitaire.

I used to consider that activity an especially pointless way to waste time, until not long ago I upgraded my computer setup with *Windows,* which includes a solitaire game. I tried it and became guiltily addicted. It took only a minute or so to play, because the virtual cards on the screen were dealt so much faster than real ones, and it was tempting—while getting ready to decide to start work— to play five or six games just to see how the cards would come out. When they fell into place, it felt like a lucky omen—though I also felt like an idiot for wasting my time this way. Then I read that even Tolstoy had done it, though not, of course, with a computer. In his day people often played patience, as it was called, as a kind of parlor oracle. Tolstoy would deal out the cards while mulling over some decision. "If the patience comes out," he would say to himself, "I will do such and such." Then he'd finish the game and do what he really wanted to do whether the cards came out right or not. When I traveled to Moscow I visited Tolstoy's house and saw his writing desk, and I pictured him wasting time there in the morning, saying to himself, "If the cards come out, Natasha will marry Pierre."

The crones in the old house were very definite about how much money they wanted for it: a sum that was both excessively large and strangely precise, as if it had been dictated to them by the cards or by a Ouija board. Anyone who offered less, they angrily turned away. I thought it over for a couple of weeks. I went back to the house and photographed it. I thought about it all the time. It was like an infatuation. It was like unexpectedly befriending a woman long admired from a distance and fantasized about, but who had seemed unapproachable; now one suddenly finds her available, needy, and beset with problems. Perhaps the fantasy is better.

Many problems beset that house. It cost too much. The repairs would cost even more. Also, my wife adamantly did not like the idea of living next to a cemetery.

And of course, the house was haunted. That is to say, it was still suffused with the astronomer's character. It could never be my house, or our house; it would always be *his* house. If I renovated it according to my tastes, I would clash with his spirit. If I restored it to his, as the conscientious owner of a historic landmark, I would become a sort of live-in curator.

That is what happened to the man who eventually did buy it. He was the only one who would meet the crones' price. He too had become obsessed, more selflessly and learnedly than I. It became his mission to research every available fact about the astronomer's life and the house's history.

Guided by old documents and photographs, he restored the house as exactly as he could to the way he believed it had appeared when it was new. He tore off the crumbling shingles and replaced them with the board-and-batten siding shown in the photographs, and painted it black and brown, as contemporary descriptions had it. He filled it with antique furniture from the astronomer's era.

But the closer he approached the original owner's conception, the less it seemed to be a haunted house. It became a paradox: a 130-year-old new house. The neighbors didn't like it. They were used to its gentle decrepitude when the hags lived there; now the black and brown board-and-batten struck them as garish, never mind that photos proved it had started out that way. The house looked smaller and less mysterious than before, no longer in community with the graveyard. It seemed, finally, less real—and less a place in which to situate a story. The accretion and deterioration of a century, part of a living process of change, were cleared away in favor of objects that recreated the facts of a century ago but not their life and meaning, for no one can restore the way they were perceived and lived with then.

Historic restoration is a paradoxical quest—like the original-instrument movement in classical music, which aims for the sounds of Mozart's time but can't give us its ears. If the musicologically correct performance strikes us as refreshing, with its textures leaner and tempos faster than those we were accustomed to, that is really a reflection of our own changing taste, which prefers clarity now, and speed, over gravity.

No doubt the house restorer's version reflected something important to himself, a personal, antiquarian virtual reality; and he seemed happy and proud when he showed it to me. But in my view it had become a sort of elegant simulacrum. In any event, when the house is haunted again, a century from now, it will be his shade and not the astronomer's that wanders there.

I began looking at other houses that had towers on them, having become fixated with the idea of a tower. One had belonged to a writer who published a best-selling novel and got stuck trying to produce a second, so stuck that he suffered a nervous breakdown in that very house, ended his marriage, and sold the place. It over-looked, moreover, a parking lot full of school buses—for me a far bleaker prospect than gravestones.

In another, the owner explained that he was selling the house because it made him sneeze. He was allergic to horsehair, which he said the nineteenth-century builders had put in the walls as insulation. I felt my nose begin to tickle.

All the houses had something wrong with them. Finally I began making drawings of houses with towers, because I was set on having an office in a tower; and I bought a building lot on a hill in the woods. The spot was about a mile due south of the astronomer's house; there was even a trail connecting the two, though interrupted now by the backyards of a new subdivision. This north-south line also turned out to intersect, more or less, the horsehair house, the blocked writer's house, my best friends' house, and two other houses I had considered buying. Extending it farther north, across Long Island Sound, it encompassed the town in Connecticut where I had spent four years at boarding school, and also the village in Vermont where my grandparents had lived.

Through this discovery, I arrived at the concept of psychic longitude. Take a map, mark a number of spots that have been significant in your life, and draw a line connecting them. If it is a straight line, that is your psychic longitude. Extend the line in its chronological direction to see what places the future may have in store for you (mine points across the sea to Haiti and Venezuela). Or perhaps the connection does not form a line, but a circle. Or a letter. Or several letters that begin a message.

I call this a virtual theory. A virtual theory is a kind of story that might as well be true and that improves on an otherwise inexplicable or unremarkable truth. (Why do men sing in the shower? Where do colds come from? Why don't travel writers get old? Why did Nixon tape himself? What is the Devil's phone number? There are chapters in this book that answer each of these questions.) It is the flip side of my theme, which is the phantom, the imposter, the thing or place that is other than what it appears to be.

My drawings of houses with towers took me back to Vermont, on the line of psychic longitude, to an owner-builder school where I took a two-week crash course in house design. I completed a rough plan and showed it to the local building inspector. He said no to the tower—he, the bureaucrat, enemy of dreams. It exceeded his height restriction. So the house I built has no tower after all; only the stump of one, which ends in a small attic-level deck, where I mount my telescope and look at the rings of Saturn. Yet the tower is still there in the concept that made me build the house. I see it, if no one else can. And in the attic, behind my virtual tower, is my desk and the computer I am writing on.

An owner-designed house is prehaunted. I intend to stay here in one form or another for the next thousand years—or until someone comes along and restores the place. On my bedroom wall is a lithograph by Odilon Redon, the artist of dreams, from a series called *The Haunted House*. It is almost entirely black, Redon's favorite color, except for the shadowy hint of a staircase and a sourceless glow that hangs in the air, casting its rays on the door. It is a bit like the glow of a computer screen in a darkened room. The picture has a caption: "I see a glimmer large and pale." In my living room is Redon's portrait of the Devil, from a series illustrating Flaubert's *The Temptation of Saint Anthony*. This Devil is young, handsome, and highly intelligent. He looks worried. Around his head is a reverse halo, an emanation of darkness. One of his black, scaly wings protrudes behind it. He looks forward, past the viewer. He is thinking. Saint Anthony stands behind him, looking at the ground. This picture is captioned: "Anthony: 'What is the object of all this?' The Devil: 'There is no object.' "

When I built my house, I thought of it as a living thing. The windows were the eyes. The plumbing was the circulatory system. The wiring was the nerve connections. The studs and beams were the bones. The books and pictures were the soul. The cesspool was . . . and so on. I was the mind. Now I think of the house sometimes as a computer. The pictures, books, and music are the software. The cats are also software. The bed is the processing board. I am the operating system.

Today I can pretend that the house is like a computer, or more sensibly report that it contains one. I can imagine that the ghost of a house haunts the computer. Or perhaps it is the Devil. Ten years ago these things would never have occurred to me. Nor would the idea of owning a computer in the first place. Ten years from now we will be saying and doing things that are inconceivable today—because of electronic technology. We and our language are in the early, fragmentary stage of a revolution.

It is an imagination machine that whirs on my desk. I do not understand how it works (therefore it is not unreasonable to locate a ghost in it), but I can count on it to harbor and display all manner of things: a book and the means to write one, a chessboard and a formidable opponent, a Scrabble set and an opponent I can still beat, a checkbook, a deck of cards, a calculator, a map, and an orrery—an astronomical program called *Dance of the Planets,* which the astronomer's shade criticizes over my shoulder.

The personal computer becomes more and more personal; over time, almost without thinking about it, the user configures its memory in ways that are as uniquely his own as the interior of his house. It is not yet sentient, not yet haunting. Not yet. And it has not yet joined forces with various kindred objects that also exist in the house.

I switch on the light and set the thermostat. I check the answering machine. I put a CD on the stereo. I turn on the computer and write a column (which I may revise later as a chapter in this book). I print it. Perhaps I make a photocopy. I fax it to my newspaper. Different actions, different machines.

Already the printer, the copier, and the fax are evolving convergently. Had I waited a year or two, I could have bought one machine instead of three. A few years more, and everything will be connected. Houses will be wired into universal machines, which will contain libraries of text, music, and videos, as well as the owner's work, the controls for the house's environment, and perhaps a collection of favorite recipes interfacing with a robot chef in the kitchen.

Rather than say that the computer is in the house, we may say that it *is* the house, or even that the house is in the computer, for the walls will be hung with holographic screens that display virtual-reality images of ideal interiors and artwork from the computer's memory, tailored to the owner's taste. We can live in virtual palaces. But when the hard drive crashes, or a virus strikes, the Devil knows what will appear on the walls; accustomed to the environment of our virtual dream house, we will feel suddenly catapulted into Hell.

Properly functioning, and perfected with upgrades that more and more emulate human intelligence, the universal house machine will be like an obedient, loving servant who knows every detail of our lives and preferences and is always ready to anticipate our desires. It will speak to us, reminding us of appointments and commiserating over our problems. It will serve up images and sounds that soothe and entice us. It will help us make decisions. It will figure out our thoughts and dreams. It will be a kind of alter ego. When we are not home, it will welcome callers and visitors in our voice and style. And when we die, it will not. Unless our heirs reprogram the machine, it will go on recreating our personality forever. When visitors come, it will presume to give them messages in our name. It will be the technological realization of the haunted house.

Manuscripts
Don't Burn

Thoughts are things, said the philosopher in the Sag Harbor graveyard. As a writer, speaking of words, I would go further. Words are more real than things. They exist somewhere beyond the visible world, to be received in moments of pure concentration, and cannot be destroyed.

But the written word is also a perishable commodity: black marks on paper (or blips on magnetic disks). Writers stand between eternity and the recycling bin. Books can be forgotten, rejected, remaindered, ignored, eaten by computer bugs, printed on crumbling acidic paper, lost, censored, suppressed, and burned, to name a few of their perils.

Like rare wildlife, like the cranes of Afghanistan and the tigers of Cambodia, rare books are at risk in the crossfire of war: those of the University of Bucharest, for example. Among the 300,000 volumes that burned up when the secret police set fire to the library, perhaps there were some of which no other copies existed, which are now and forever extinct. For we who love books, this thought is unbearable. They must somehow still exist, immaculate and immortal, in some great Platonic library, the library of Heaven, where scholars can go when they die.

Iris Murdoch writes each of her magnificent novels

in longhand and carries the completed manuscript, the only copy, in a paper bag from her home in Oxford to her publisher in London. I worry about this. Imagine: a thief grabs the bag and runs. Later, finding only papers inside, he throws it away in disgust. The book disappears. Hardly born yet, it's already extinct. The thought is unbearable. Surely the book exists. Every book ever written exists, whether we can physically locate it or not. That is how I feel about it.

(Or imagine: Iris Murdoch, having lost the novel, goes home and writes it again. This manuscript she sends to her publisher in an armored car. The book is read by millions. Meanwhile, the manuscript the thief stole lies buried in a garbage dump. Fifty years later, by chance, somebody digs it out and shows it to a scholar, who compares the two versions and finds that (a) they are identical, word for word; (b) they are like successive drafts of the same book; or (c) they are totally different. My heart votes for a. My brain inclines to b or c. Or another scenario: the fellow who digs up the manuscript can't read, and he throws it back in the pit, where it remains forever. Its phantom existence has blinked out again. The second version remains the only one, which readers experience as unique, inevitable, the volume on file in the library of heaven.)

I know a literary agent who left the only copy of a client's manuscript in a taxi (it was never found) and a writer who saw a chapter of his book vanish abruptly from his computer's screen and memory. Another lost her whole book when the Oakland fire consumed her computer, backup disks, and printouts.

There is a project in Egypt to build a new library in Alexandria, at the site of the one that burned down in antiquity. If not for that fire, there might be additional volumes by writers like Sophocles and Euripides, maybe even better ones, in bookstores and libraries today.

A classics scholar would sell his soul to the Devil for a chance to browse in the original library. Such is the magic we attribute to books, to the idea of their immortality, that this bargain sounds plausible.

And sometimes words do return from seeming extinction, not always for the best. Pedants love to disinter early drafts and letters whose authors believed them safely discarded. Occasionally a lost masterpiece reappears.

The novel *Life and Fate,* a Soviet-era emulation of *War and Peace,* disappeared in 1960. The unpublished manuscript was, in effect, arrested; the KGB confiscated every copy. For the author, Vasily Grossman, this was even worse than if he had been arrested himself. His life's work had been taken away—apparently to be destroyed. He died in 1964 without knowing if the novel still existed. Ten years later a microfilm copy surfaced in the west, and today you can go to your local bookshop and buy a translation (still lacking a few passages that were missing from the microfilm, that are still in the phantom realm).

When I traveled to St. Petersburg, I visited a literary archive where thousands of rare and even bizarre manuscripts were kept (rather haphazardly) in manila folders. Among those the librarian pulled out and laid on her desk for her visitors to see were a peremptory letter from Czar Peter the Great ("Come see me at once!" it said), some envelopes on which Dostoyevsky had doodled faces and jotted notes for *The Brothers Karamazov,* and the suicide letter of the poet Esenin, penned in his own blood.

Another manuscript, which consisted of tiny shreds laboriously sewn together, had been among the writings that Nikolai Gogol set out to destroy when he lost his mind and decided that literature was worthless and blasphemous. Having once written a paper on Gogol, I thought he had burned everything, but it turned out that some of his work, at least, he merely tore to shreds and threw away.

That would have been the end of that, but for a local peasant woman who happened to be making pillows. She found the shreds in the garbage and used them to stuff the pillows. After Gogol's death, an aristocrat who admired his work sleuthed out those pillows and bought them. He hired scholars to try to piece the contents back together.

They couldn't. He got rid of the scholars and brought in other workers, villagers from his estate, who, he reasoned, wouldn't be distracted by the urge to read the fragments—who would treat the job as an abstract puzzle. These people, who finally reassembled the manuscript, were illiterate.

Whether it was worth the trouble, as literature, I don't know. Never mind. I like the miraculous element in this story. Here is a piece of writing that appeared to perish, as its distraught author intended it to do—until a strange and paradoxical sequence of events brought it back from extinction.

I like to believe that books can't die. "Manuscripts don't burn." The line is from another Russian novel, Mikhail Bulgakov's *The Master and Margarita*. Bulgakov, who lived in Stalin's time, burned the only manuscript copy of this novel in a fit of despair. But later he relented and wrote it again. It was almost finished at the time of his death, but it wasn't published for another quarter-century.

Its main character, the master, is also the author of an

unpublished novel (about Christ and Pontius Pilate), for which he is persecuted, and which, despairing, he burns. Near the end of Bulgakov's book, the Devil, who has been visiting Moscow in the guise of a magician named Woland, asks to see the master's book.

"Unfortunately I cannot show it to you," replied the master, "because I burned it in my stove."

"I'm sorry but I don't believe you," said Woland. "You can't have. Manuscripts don't burn." He turned to Behemoth [his cat] and said, "Come on, Behemoth, give me the novel."

The cat jumped down from its chair, and where he had been sitting was a pile of manuscripts. With a bow the cat handed the top copy to Woland. . . .

Virus Zero

If manuscripts don't burn, at least when the Devil takes a hand, then neither should computers crash. But Lucifer's legions are not always the writer's friends. In precomputer days the editor at my newspaper would blame typos on "the printer's devil." Today, when popular dread has assumed a medical rather than theological form, we call it something else: a bug, or a virus.

The most notorious of viruses was perversely named after an artist, albeit one of diabolical genius: Michelangelo. The hackers who concoct them proceed from deviltry, an urge to cause havoc, destruction, and grief in artistically ingenious ways.

Where old-fashioned vandals burned libraries and looted material wealth, these techies target the magnetic repositories of information which constitute virtual wealth. So far their attacks have been random. But suppose they join forces with terrorists. They have already caused such panic, these cyberspace outlaws whose mischief is innocent of politics; imagine what will happen when radical revolutionaries go on line.

Imagine, for instance, some ferociously utopian hacker who, on the theory that money is the root of all evil, puts his or her programming genius to work getting rid of it. Money. All of it, everywhere.

Before computers, this was impossible. Money used to be something you could touch and carry around and hide. The only revolutionary who seriously tried to abolish money was Cambodia's Pol Pot. Despite his extreme tactics many Cambodians managed to bury their savings, in the form of gold—to be retrieved, if they survived, after the reign of terror had passed.

In the postindustrial West, however, money has become more and more abstract. Gold (or silver or cowrie shells) was the ancient first stage of abstraction, a portable substitute for the actual goods to be bartered. Then came bank notes, less trouble to carry around than ingots or coins and still representing the existence of actual gold or silver that was kept in some bank vault to back their value.

Those were replaced in this century by bank notes that no longer had any tangible backing—only their own reputation backed by that of the government. Everyone went on agreeing to accept these numbered pieces of paper in exchange for goods, in the belief that everyone else would do so, and most were ready to hand them over to banks in the belief that the bankers would keep accurate accounts of who owned what and would hand back equivalent pieces of paper on demand.

This system enabled the invention of checks, with which people wrote their own personal money, which was accepted in the belief that it was backed by actual government money in the check writer's bank account. Checks further speeded up the economy, as they could be mailed as well as carried from place to place.

Today we have arrived at an even higher level of abstraction: electrons. The bank notes that substituted for the gold that substituted for the goods are in turn substituted for by computerized bank records, by the magnetic strips on credit cards and ATM cards, and by the electric currents that convey information about transactions from shop to credit card company or from bank to bank with lightning speed along telephone wires.

Never has money moved so fast, nor so hypothetically. Only the poor, or those with illicit gains to hide, rely exclusively on cash. The more money people have, the less likely they are actually to see it or touch it. Wealth inheres in a little black stripe on a piece of plastic and in the magnetic patterns that represent numbers in the computer memories of the banking system.

This has given rise to a new class of criminal, who steals by tampering with the electrons. Rather than the old physical work of walking into a bank with a gun and carrying off bundles of bank notes, a thief with the right programming skills need only gain access to the right computer: a more humane and devious form of bank robbery in which no one gets shot and, often, no one gets caught.

In one subtle heist, a larcenous cyberpunk invaded a bank's computer and altered the program that credited account holders with the interest on their deposits. Normally the computer would round fractions of a cent up or down to the nearest whole cent. The hacker instructed it to round every payment down to the lower cent, and to deposit the leftover fractions of cents in his own account. He figured that no one would ever notice this, and, in the years before he was somehow caught, the fractions of cents he siphoned off daily from the bank's many thousands of accounts added up to a lot of money.

By the same electronic token, government can do the tampering. I myself was a victim, several years ago, in the course of a dispute with the Internal Revenue Service.

One day my bank's cash machine failed to respond to the usual ritual of dipping the ATM card and typing the access code. According to the machine, my balance was now zero. The IRS had done this, electronically seizing my account as a hostage to its claim.

At least one dystopian novelist has recognized the possibilities here. In Margaret Atwood's *The Handmaid's Tale,* religious fundamentalists carry out a putsch against the U.S. government and, as a first step in their male-chauvinist program, cause the banking system's computers to abolish all accounts whose owners are female.

Which brings me back to my hypothetical Pol Pot virus. There is at work even today, let's imagine, a brilliant hacker motivated by an ideology of extreme-radical egalitarianism. He is able to gain access to a computer in a bank somewhere, into which he introduces an insidious software program that, over time, in the course of electronic fund transfers from bank to bank, infects every computer in the capitalist world's monetary system.

On a certain date—May Day, let's say—the virus causes the entire system to crash. Every bank balance, every credit card balance, every electronically recorded account balance of any kind whatever, suddenly changes to zero. All the money in the developed world disappears, except for whatever negligible amount of cash people happen to be carrying in their wallets that day.

The Dow Jones average is zero. The federal budget is zero, but so is the deficit. The rich are aghast. They demand that all the bank accounts and brokerage accounts and so on be reconstructed from the paper trail of checks and deposit slips and so forth. But there are trillions of these pieces of paper; the job would take years.

Meanwhile the middle class, finding its debts

changed to zero, and the poor, lacking bank accounts in the first place, are not at all unhappy with the new state of affairs. They don't see why the government should go to all the trouble of sifting through those trillions of documents. Much simpler just to start over and divide the wealth equally. The government doesn't see it that way, of course, but because the virus has temporarily made it impossible for special interests to make campaign contributions, the incumbents are all voted out. The economy begins anew with everyone at the same starting line.

Can it happen? I don't see why not. Watch your ATM machine and see.

Satan's Cellar

Another kind of virus comes straight from the Devil himself. We insult him by calling it the common cold. There's nothing common about it, he says. Each miserable cold is miserable in its own way. Each has its own style, weight, texture, flavor, and sonority. In their perverse way, colds are as various as wines.

The Devil keeps them in his cellar, in bottles. He collects every variety and vintage of virus with a connoisseur's gusto. "Send up a bottle of Chateau Ah-Choo '92," he orders. "Ah, a good year. Such misery, such impudence! And how the bouquet does linger, and linger."

He sips a glass of this and a glass of that, savoring the subtleties of distress. There are so many colds for him to choose from, so many exquisite symptoms. There are head colds and throat colds, coughs and wheezes, sniffles and sneezes. There are chest colds and nose colds, stuffy or streaming; explosive colds, percussive colds, and those that honk and blare. There are colds that make you dizzy, colds that make you glum, colds that make your bones ache, colds that make you numb. There are those that make your ears throb, those that make your eyes sting, some that curdle your brain, some that make you croak like a frog, and some that go on and on and almost break your heart.

"Good!" says the Devil when he has made his choice. "I'll send him a case of this!" He snaps his fingers and a goblin delivery boy comes running. He takes out a card that reads "Seasons Greetings" and writes a name and address: mine, or yours.

"How're you doing?" people ask me the next day. Maybe they are spies for the Devil.

"Oh, fighting a cold," I answer. Day after day I fight it. And it fights back. I fight it with vitamin C, chicken soup, oranges, cough syrup, honeyed tea, Contac, cognac, and will power. The Devil just laughs. This is no common ailment—the kind there's a cure for. This comes straight from Satan's own cellar.

I fight—and sooner or later I yield. So much for will power. The cold has won. I take to my bed. I become like a cat, snoozing fitfully round the clock. I forget what day it is. I dream the same dream over and over.

The Buddha, on his wanderings, comes one day to a river crossing, where, waiting for the ferry, he meets a holy man. The holy man reveals that, after a prodigious effort of spiritual concentration, he has mastered the art of walking on water. He is about to demonstrate this skill when the Buddha interjects: "Why bother? Here comes the ferry, and the fare's only a nickel!"

And I dream of the philosopher who asked: "What is the best thing the rat can do when he is caught in the trap?"

His answer: "Eat the cheese."

In the end, there is something voluptuous about a really bad cold, the kind that offers no way out but to curl up under a quilt and sleep and wait.

After which, after a day or two or three of weird, repetitive dreams (Buddha on a ferryboat, rats in a trap),

I begin lightheadedly to stir. It turns out that I am alive after all. I am free again. I've somehow molted. I go back to my daily routine, dazed but renewed. I have survived—and, in a perverse way, luxuriated in—my Stygian interlude.

The Devil moves on. He considers that '93 has been a very good year, so far; a very fine vintage. A good year for colds and for other of his activities, too.

But he's never satisfied. He believes in progress. The worst is yet to come, he says. The year is still young.

TWILIGHT *of the* GLUTTONS

Government
Time

November is the Devil's favorite month, when, cheered by Halloween, he uncorks his most potent colds and, abetted by the federal government, shrouds the land with darkness.

"No sun, no moon, no warmth, no joy, November." So went the refrain of a lugubrious poem I learned in school and remember each year while setting the clocks back.

It could be worse. This could be Finland with its ceaseless winter night, where it doesn't matter how you set the clocks, because it's always going to be dark anyway. If Hemingway had been Finnish he'd have written *Nor Does the Sun Rise*. I once asked a stewardess on a Finnair flight what people in Helsinki do in the winter. "We get very sad," she said.

Too bad we aren't descended from bears. These dwindling dreary grey November days, wouldn't you really rather be a bear, with a guilt-free fur coat, a belly full of salmon, and a biological clock that says it's time to hibernate?

Imagine you're *Ursus sapiens,* getting up from Thanksgiving dinner, turning on the answering machine, turning down the thermostat, and turning in for a good long nap, I mean a *long* nap. You've piled on the down comforters. You've set the alarm for March 21. "Sweet dreams," you say. "See you in the spring."

No such luck. It's still November in the real world. The wind howls, cold rain splats against the window-panes, and the leaves you raked off the lawn yesterday have all blown back again. You put on a sweater. You put on another sweater. You open the fuel bill and see how strife in a faraway hot desert has made it jump.

And the nights grow longer. Already in October, by the time you were ready for certain evening rituals, like going for a jog, cutting some wood, or watching the sunset with a martini, it was too late. It was dark already.

And then what happened? Government stepped in. The function of government is to wait until a situation has gotten pretty bad and then intervene to make it worse.

"Not enough daylight?" says government. "Dark at six o'clock already? Yeah, that's too bad. Tell you what. We'll make a law. Everybody turn their clocks back one hour."

And we do. We may cheat on taxes and speed limits, but when it comes to time we're scrupulous. Nobody refuses to set their clocks back. Nobody goes on strike against standard time. Nobody makes the rational move of setting their clocks *ahead* an hour.

We all traipse obediently around looking for clocks and watches to set back: in the kitchen and the car, on the radio, the stove, the calculator, the computer, the VCR, and all the other gadgets that have clocks nowadays. I set back everything but the cats. How do you reset a cat? They miaow at what their biological clocks still say is their regular dinnertime of six, unaware that the government now says it's five.

So the nights fall even sooner than they would have if government had stayed out of it. And why? Who benefits? I've tried to come up with some answers:

1. Lightbulb manufacturers.
2. Electric utilities.
3. Oil producers.
4. Trick-or-treaters.
5. Astronomers.

The prime suspect is number three, the most powerful of these lobbies. Standard time, the kind with the short evenings, must have been named after Standard Oil.

Only once did government come to its senses—in the winter of 1973–74, when daylight saving time, the good kind, was extended year-round to save energy. That was during a Mideast oil crisis and the heyday of the solar lobby. Then everyone forgot about it. We went back to fiddling with our clocks each fall and spring.

What happened? A conspiracy to sell more lightbulbs, oil, and Halloween masks? Or just another of those things government does that make no sense at all?

The Turkey

So I'm thinking about bears again, longing for their talent of hibernating. Instead I have Thanksgiving. I hunker down in my den, with my mate and cubs and kin, and devour the largest creature that can fit in my oven, stuffing myself into a state of blissful drowsiness.

That creature is the turkey—the bloated bird whose exaggerated proportions parody the chickens of summer. The bigger the better. The rest of the year I seldom think of turkeys, except as a sandwich ingredient or a term of abuse, as in "Who elected that turkey?" or "Why would she want to go out with such a turkey?"

But in the waning days of November I crave the hugest thing I can feasibly cook, like a bruin putting away bulk against a long winter's sleep. Were I a Lapp or Siberian, it would be wild boar or reindeer. Were I a Bedouin, celebrating Thanksgiving around an open fire, the main course would be a stuffed camel. But who needs Thanksgiving in the Sahara, which knows not the curse of our northern November, the morbidity of grey skies and fallen leaves and premature nights, and the nostalgia for ursine slumber?

Had Thanksgiving originated with eastern Long Island's Bonackers, the fishermen who are descended from the area's seventeenth-century settlers—then the traditional course would be a striped bass, their prize catch, a lovelier creature by far than the misshapen turkey. But we follow the landward-looking and unaesthetic Massachusetts Puritans. They did not know, perhaps, about the turkey's morals. He is a polygamous bird, according to my encyclopedia, which also explains that his name has nothing to do with the country Turkey, but instead "derives from its 'turk-turk' call."

Turk-turk! My neighbor Joe Pintauro, who wrote a play about the Bonackers (based on the book *Men's Lives* by another neighbor, Peter Matthiessen), also thinks about turkeys. He therefore wrote a skit about a family of giant turkeys who gather on Thanksgiving Day for a feast of stuffed human. That seems fair. No one else, except vegetarians, spares much sympathy for the community of turkeys, among whom November 26 is the day that lives in infamy.

I'll take a drumstick anyway, with plenty of stuffing and gravy and a big dollop of cranberry sauce. There's little else to be thankful for in November. This holiday is perversely named. It's like saying, "Well, it's November, it's cold and dark and wet, and winter is coming, it's only going to get colder and darker and ever more grim, but let's deny all that and just be thankful for this chance to eat lots of turkey." An apter name would be Avoidance Day, or Denialgiving.

It would defeat the purpose, however, to speak of having the family over for Denialgiving dinner. So Thanksgiving it is—thanks that even in godawful November we can be warm and gluttonous together. I myself would have scheduled Thanksgiving in April. The spring is when I sincerely do feel that way. I can't imagine where T. S. Eliot was coming from. November is the cruelest month.

Like a bear, anyway, I stuff myself today, then waddle home to snooze. If only I could snooze till April. The wintrier the country, the greater its affinity with bears. The bear has always characterized Russia, in the way that Britain has been represented as a lion, China as a dragon, France as a pretty girl, and the United States as an eagle (though Benjamin Franklin proposed the turkey).

The bear is a popular symbol in a land that traditionally passed its harsh winters huddled idly beside the peasant stove, and its short summers in a frenzy of food gathering, so that its economic practices ever since have been marked by alternating periods of furious activity and fatalistic sloth.

Mischa the bear was the Moscow Olympic mascot. And a favorite spectacle in Moscow today is a show called the Battling Bruins—trained bears on skates, playing ice hockey.

In America, bears have a similar dual reputation: on the one hand the macho grizzly, on the other the somnolent honey slurper. Apparently the latter is more accurate. Take the notorious mugger bears of the Appalachians. Yes, it's true; these are bears that like to terrify hikers at a certain spot on the Appalachian Trail, charging at them with seeming ferocity. They do this because they have learned that the hikers, while fleeing, always throw down their backpacks so as to run away faster. Then the bears stop and ransack the backpacks. It's not haunch of hiker they hunger for, but the peanut butter and jelly sandwiches they know are in the packs.

The grizzly's grisly image was thoroughly deflated by a scientific study at Yosemite, which established that the wild bears there subsist mainly on a diet of moths. Yes moths.

Disillusioned, I pictured Papa Bear, Mama Bear, et al. sitting down to their Thanksgiving feast with plates piled high with wispy white moths. "Have some more moth, dear," says she. "Pass the honey, honey," he yawns. "Almost time for my nice long, long, long nap."

Gingerbread Man

I eat, therefore I am. Infants arrive in the world with the urge to eat it. Whatever they can grab they pull toward their tiny mouths, until they are taught their first fact of life: you can't eat it all.

"Hansel and Gretel" is about breaking that injunction. Returning to a state in which everything looks good to eat, the children find to their horror that so do they. But Christmas—with its emphasis on feasting and consuming and its imagery of edible ornaments—also invites us back to that omnivorous infant state. Christmas says it's all right to go home to a gingerbread house for a day, but "Hansel and Gretel" says don't stay.

There is a street in my town where I imagine it is always Christmas. It is called Gingerbread Lane. Here I imagine a December tale. Here a hungry traveler sniffs the air, recognizes a bewitching aroma—his favorite childhood treat, whatever it was—and follows his nose to the house on Gingerbread Lane.

It's a big, warm house, redolent of baking and roasting, a haven for a cold and hungry wanderer like me. I knock on the door, it swings open, and I enter, shaking the frosting from my boots. There's a visitor's book by the door, open for me to sign. There's a message written in the book, and this is what it says: "Welcome, weary traveler, to the Gingerbread House. Eat your fill, and stay as long as you like. You will never hunger again, nor need to go out for groceries, for everything in the house is delicious, from the gingerbread rafters to the peppermint doorknobs, and there's enough to last your lifetime."

There's more writing on the page. It looks like icing on a cake. "A general confectioner built this house," it says,

after the town planners approved the recipe and issued a baking permit. First came the bulldozer, cutting into the fudgy loam; then the truck with the big blender on its back, which mixed the batter for the foundation and poured it into a mold in the ground.

Next came the framing crew with the gingerbread studs and rafters, joined with cloves, and the roofers with bundles of wafers for shingles. The mason built a marzipan chimney. The plumber installed licorice pipes and caramel fixtures. And when the insulation crew had made the house nice and snug with angel-cake batts and taffy caulk, along came the drywall crew with sheetrock candy and marshmallow spackle.

The owner had all kinds of decisions to make: what flavor of kitchen tile, lemon or cherry? Butterscotch grout, or vanilla? Walnut wainscotting? Or pecan? How about coconut cabinets? Or almond ones? What flavor, hungry traveler, would you prefer?

The stairs are railed with candy canes, the patio is paved with peanut brittle, the windows are double-pane sugar frost. The paint job is tasteful: honey in the bedroom, coffee in the den. When the last piece of chocolate trim was in place, the house was ready for a visit from the baking inspector, who poked everything with his fork, took a bite of this and that, and issued the certificate of edibility.

You'll find it, dear traveler, a cozy house, with its maple sugar furniture, cotton candy stuffed quilts, and brandy flambé heating system. It's all finished now, just in time for Christmas—for a visit from a cold and hungry wanderer like you. You're welcome to settle in as long as you like. All your life, even.

Signed: The Owner (can you guess who I am?)

I sniff the binding of the visitor's book. It's made of gingerbread. I wonder who it was who wrote this letter, and who hired the general confectioner to build the gingerbread house to lure a hungry wanderer like me. Was it Santa? Was it the Devil? Or was it the witch from "Hansel and Gretel"?

I stay. In the gingerbread house I am never hungry, never cold. The house is always warm and tasty. Outside it is always snowing. Why should I leave?

And one day I look in a sugar-glazed mirror and see not my accustomed reflection but something magically, enticingly transformed, something doomed yet frozen in a smile: a gingerbread man.

The Lobster Trees

Eating is an ambiguously sensual and savage act at any season. Declining a serving of lobster at a beach picnic July 4, I recalled the day two months earlier, in Korea, when I was invited to a dog restaurant. I considered accepting in the scientific spirit of trying everything once, as I had already done with the Korean delicacy known as live octopus. Lobsters, I admit, I have eaten more than once, until one night last year I had a disturbing dream about lobster trees.

Dog owners may object to the parallel, but lobsters have always struck me as wise-looking animals. The French poet Gérard de Nerval kept one as a pet and took it for walks in the park, boasting that it never barked and that it understood the secrets of the deep.

I associate lobsters with a tender-hearted woman I once met at a party. She had bought eight of them one day, taken them home, and set the water boiling. Then, reflecting on what she was about to do, she burst into tears. She drove the lobsters to a beach and set them free. While she fondly watched them march down to the water, her seven eager guests were turning up at her house, wondering where she was, not knowing their festive meal was down to French fries and melted butter.

I seem to remember an article in *Science Times* a

while back that established that lobsters are highly gregarious creatures. They like to stroll along the ocean floor and pay social calls on one another, schmoozing in their briny burrows. At least that's the way I remember it. My lobster-eating friends at the picnic claimed that I either made it up or dreamed it, and that lobsters are in fact little devils—nasty cannibals who deserve everything we do to them.

Maybe so. A newspaper colleague, a fishing reporter, once interviewed a lobsterman who spoke of the importance of timing in retrieving his traps. If he waited too long, the trap would turn out to contain, instead of many lobsters, only one—which he called "the winner." The reason lobsters are so delicious, according to the succulently circular logic of my picnic companions, is that the food they themselves eat is so delicious: other lobsters.

A decision to eat is a struggle between appetite and curiosity, on the one side, and compassion and disgust on the other. I gave up hot dogs years ago because of several sentences in an article in *New York* magazine. The article was a collection of reminiscences by a former policeman who had served in the South Bronx precinct house known as Fort Apache. On patrol late one night, he claimed, he had spotted a flatbed truck carrying what he took to be the heftiest dead man he had ever seen, a veritable hunk. On closer inspection, it turned out to be a skinned gorilla, which had expired of natural causes in some zoo and was being transported under cover of night to a Bronx frankfurter plant.

Although the late Jimmy Hoffa was said to have been similarly recycled in a hamburger plant, I went on eating burgers, figuring there was only about one chance in a billion that the specific Big Mac I was munching would be one of those among which the murder evidence had been thus dispersed. I stopped after reading an article in *Mother Jones* about what goes on at beef packing plants and what things routinely get tossed into the grinding machines. Not just the occasional gorilla and Teamster boss.

A lobster shell, naturally, is sure to contain the lobster, the whole lobster, and nothing but the lobster. For truth in packaging and freshness, it has few rivals. And it demands of those who cook it an unflinching consistency—as opposed to the chicken, for example, whose aficionados leave the dirty work to Mr. Perdue. The deed, however, always left me haunted by weird imaginings: reincarnation as a lobster (the lobster god's revenge) or a science fiction scenario in which giant intelligent lobster-beings toss live humans into the bubbling cauldron.

The quest for freshness leads inexorably to the border of savagery, beyond which lies the delight of the shark or wolf that gobbles live prey. In Seoul's vast fish market are counters where one can sit down to a snack of live octopus or live prawns. Order octopus, and the waitress plucks one from a tank and—bang bang bang—briskly chops it up in front of you. At that point, it is perhaps a theological question whether the creature that was swimming in the tank five seconds ago is still a living organism—but if not, the pieces thereof have not gotten the message, for they continue to squirm on the plate as the waitress hands it to you. It looks like Medusa's haircut.

And it tastes sensational. Nothing was ever fresher than this tingling clarity of the deep. It is the far side of sashimi. Yes, despite my recent forbearance toward lobster, I did, as a polite guest and scientist, try both the octopus and the prawn (which the eater is supposed to kill himself, by breaking off its head, though my Korean friend did that for me). And who are you, squeamish reader, to protest—you who avidly slurp, off the half-shell, clams and oysters that are still alive in all the fullness of their clammy and oysterish lives until the very instant your teeth gnash into their poor soft bodies?

I was more reluctant, however, to sample dog, even when assured that it was served in a kind of stew, so that you wouldn't know it was dog if, so to speak, you didn't know. Also, I'd happened to walk through a section of the Seoul market district where dog butcher shops are clustered, and where on the sidewalk dogs wait packed in crates, like chickens, while cuts of their slaughtered brethren hang nearby.

So when my friend's father offered to take me to a dog restaurant I demurred with some observations about the special feeling that all Americans have toward that species. He replied that these dogs were more analogous to cows or pigs: a special breed that is raised on farms specifically for eating, as distinct from the other kinds of dogs that Koreans keep as pets. Indeed, one sees many dogs cheerfully wandering the residential streets of Seoul, in no apparent danger of ending up in someone's cooking pot. Even at the canine meat market I saw one of these free dogs, placidly dozing in front of a shop, unmoved by the plight of his crated peers: the butcher's pet, safe in his traitorous collar.

People who have tasted dog, my host said, swear it is so good they never want to eat any other kind of meat again. He'd taken some American business colleagues to the dog restaurant, and they liked it so much they went back on their own the next day. I'd been reading a book by a British travel writer who walked the length of Korea; unlike me, he tried dog, and he said it was pretty good, although he was oppressed for a long time after by the irrational thought that, when he got back to England, his own dog would somehow smell it on his breath and never be his friend again.

My host added that he himself could imagine nothing more repulsive than the idea of eating snails—yet he had heard that people in France did so with gusto, and he did not hold it against them.

It's just as well I didn't accept the invitation, for afterward I might have had a nightmare even worse than the one that followed my last lobster dinner. In it, I was working with a shovel, in a field below a highway bridge. It was a grey, windy, rain-spattered afternoon. I was planting lobster trees. The small black lobsters hung swaying from the branches, like bananas, ready to drop off when grown and ripe. To plant the trees it was necessary to wear thick gloves, to avoid being pinched by the claws.

This dream undoubtedly has a psychoanalytic content, which I could explore now but won't, as I am not writing a psychosexual confession. There is also a plain overt meaning: lobsters don't grow on trees; their delicacy comes at a price, which is the commission of a crime—a little murder, but a grisly one.

So I draw the line these days at lobsters, as I do at dogs and, for other reasons, hot dogs. But it is a fine line that runs through a grey area, on the other side of which clams remain, and oysters, especially oysters.

"I could eat you alive," says the lover to the beloved. And so it is with us and oysters.

The Apple

Of all foods, the most redolent of truth is the apple. Apples are symbols of wisdom, not to be trifled with. Look what happened to Eve when the Devil showed her one. I feel intuitively that the fruit of the Tree of Knowledge was an apple, even if the Bible doesn't say so and scholars argue it must have been a pomegranate or a fig. Just try to imagine Satan offering Eve a fig. No red-blooded woman would be seriously tempted by a fig, which has connotations of insignificance, as in "I don't care a fig," and prudery—the fig leaf.

It was an apple that revolutionized science, when Newton saw one fall and got to thinking about gravity. A fig wouldn't have done it, not even a Fig Newton. When a pair of California propeller heads developed a product that became the success story of the eighties, they named it the Apple. Would Banana Computer have made it? Lemon? Fig?

Apples are symbols of learning. The first sentence I learned to read was, of course, A is for apple. An apple for the teacher was an advertisement of assiduity. The teacher's pet was the apple-polisher.

Apples went both ways at my school. The apple-polisher got them back. Good conduct earned merits; five merits earned an apple, presented at Friday morning assembly by the foxy old headmaster himself. I ran for president of the fifth grade on a pledge that everyone would get an apple, and led the polls until my opponent pointed out that class presidents lacked jurisdiction over apples. I was not a serious candidate, he charged. This character issue upset the apple cart, so to speak. I went on claiming, like Nixon, that I had a secret plan, but the voters would have none of it, and I lost, 19 to 1.

Apples are symbols of youth, health, and goodness. In "The Arabian Nights" Prince Ahmed's apple is a cure for every disorder. A healthy child is apple-cheeked, the apple of everyone's eye. An apple a day keeps the doctor away.

The Norse gods stayed young by eating the apples of Iduna. Colonial codgers kept spry tippling applejack. When the Beatles left Capitol to start their own label, they named it Apple Records. King Arthur was said to dwell eternally at Avalon, which means island of apples.

For the Greeks, apples—golden ones—were an irresistible prize. Atalanta stopped for three of them and so lost her race and her maidenhood. Another golden fruit was the reward for the most beautiful, and became the apple of discord when the goddesses fell to bickering over who deserved it. The eleventh labor of Hercules was to bring back some golden apples that grew in the garden of the Hesperides.

Apples stand for honesty and perfection. When something is nicely arranged, it's in apple-pie order. Orchards are redolent of harmony in a way that potato fields or strawberry patches can never be. The builders profiled in Tracy Kidder's book *House* expressed their ideals of honesty and craftsmanship by naming their company Apple Corps. William Tell demonstrated his marksmanship by shooting an apple off his son's head, though a pear would have served as well, and a cherry, or a blueberry, would have proved him a crack shot indeed. In my hometown the Apple Bank for Savings is thriving, to the point of taking over the Sag Harbor Savings Bank, whereas a Potato Bank, or even a Strawberry Bank, might have trouble attracting depositors.

New York's boosters call it the Big Apple, not the Big Fig or the Big Enchilada. Alma-Ata, capital of Kazakhstan, means father of apples. The hero of environmentalist legend is Johnny Appleseed. The eternal verities that politicians uphold are the American flag, motherhood, and apple pie. George Washington wouldn't have been elected had he chopped down an apple tree.

You don't fool around with apples, as I learned in fifth grade, and as the International Apple Institute learned more recently. A also stands for alar, but Americans won't have it. We'll put up with a lot, in the way of A for adulteration, additives, and artifice; but when they— "they" being the people who put chemicals in things— are caught messing around with apples, that's where we draw the line.

Apples and alar made the cover of *Consumer Reports,* and when the apple industry gave up and promised to stop using the chemical, the story was on the front page of the *New York Times,* up there with Gorbachev and Bush.

It should be. The apple that is not as it appears is a symbol of disillusion: the apple of discord, the apple with a worm in it, the apple of Sodom, or Dead Sea fruit, which is lovely to behold but tastes of ashes. Getting the alar out of apples was a victory for innocence.

The Mushroom

The mushroom, on the other hand, is surely the Devil's food. Mushrooms are magical, mystical, mysterious: often phallic, sometimes fatal, occasionally hallucinogenic. They grow faster than any decent plant rightly should, appearing to sprout overnight, nourished by decay. One pictures them dotting cemeteries and battlefields. Their colors are weird, sickly, like the complexion of a ghoul. They figure in shamanistic rites in which congregants eat them and see visions. Jesus Christ, according to a blasphemous book that came out a few years ago, was actually a sacred mushroom. In the secular world, meanwhile, the most horrifying vision of all is called the mushroom cloud.

People who understand mushrooms—who can tell them apart, name them, and pick the right ones to eat—inspire me with respect and a touch of dread. Perhaps there's a trace of some ancestral memory here—of the witch doctor who knew which of two almost identical fungi could make you see glory, and which could make you dead, so that you were careful to stay on his good side. Civilization came late to Russia, which retains a mystic soulfulness and a fanatic love of mushrooms.

Two Russians came to my house and went into ecstasies at the sight of all the mushrooms at the fringe of the woods which I'd scarcely noticed before. The place, they said, reminded them of Siberia (though it wasn't even winter), and these were the same mushrooms they used to gather before they emigrated. They had different words for all of them—not Latin terms, but earthy, succulent, Russian endearments. They picked a bunch of them and told me not to worry.

The husband sat at my kitchen table wearing a look of beatific expectation while the wife did all the work. First she put the mushrooms in boiling water—to prove, she said, that they weren't poisonous. Any that were, she claimed, would turn purple. None did.

Russia is one of those countries where, generally speaking, the women do most of the work, as if they were subservient to their spoiled husbands, but even so appear stronger and more in charge than the men they pamper. They treat their husbands like big babies. This is actually the source of their power; by treating their men this way, they retain the authority of the mother who, spoon-feeding an immobile infant, is of course the boss.

Anyway, this Russian lady served her husband a big steaming bowl of my mushrooms and watched, beaming, while he slurped them up. I waited for a decent interval, to see if he would keel over, before sampling my portion. He decided that, after all, these weren't quite the same as real Russian mushrooms. They tasted similar, he said, but lacked a certain undefinable quality of soul that only mushrooms grown on good Russian soil can possess. I found them delicious, though I kept thinking of something I'd heard about certain mushrooms being both the tastiest and the deadliest, and about erroneous mushroom hunters whose best meal is also their last. But I'm still here to tell the tale.

Which is lucky, according to a lady who knows all

about mushrooms, to whom I told it later. Catastrophes have occurred, she said, when visitors from mushroom-loving countries like Russia, China, and Japan find mushrooms here that they believe, and persuade their hosts, are identical to the ones they savored at home. She also said the procedure of dropping them in boiling water to see if they turn purple is baloney.

But she found a number of mushrooms by my house that she pronounced edible (though I'll be damned if I can remember which ones they are), as well as one that she said was a close relative to a singularly deadly variety called the Avenging Angel. She picked a little pink one and invited me to experience a taste sensation. It was, she said, not the Avenging Angel relative, but a harmless *Russula silvacola*. "At least I think so," she added.

"You *think* so!!!" I spluttered. Never one to refuse an implied dare, which will be my undoing someday, I tried it anyway. It had, as she said, an extremely spicy flavor, like a chili pepper, but with a strange soapy undertone: kind of like five parts Tabasco to one part Head & Shoulders. And it lingered in my mouth for about two hours, while I continually checked myself, as I had done after the Russians' dinner, to make sure I was neither dying nor hallucinating. I'd pick some more and add it to my famous chili recipe if I were less nervous about making a mistake and offering my guests a succulent last supper of Avenging Angel Chili.

How, I wonder, do people who eat those hallucinogenic mushrooms know for sure that what they are experiencing is in fact a temporary trip and not a near-death experience? For me, that suspicion would be sure to color my hallucinations with dread and produce a bad trip. So I've never tried one. Which is just as well. I knew someone who ate them a lot, and who even used to invite his friends to magic mushroom parties, though that was before I knew him. He was a talented guy, but there was always something disconnected and spacy about him; he was not all there, in the sense that people who dropped a lot of acid in college and are now 20 years older are still often not all there. The last I heard, he was farming mushrooms in Hawaii.

Occasionally I look out my window and see a deer or a squirrel on my lawn eating a mushroom. That one, then, is safe to eat, I think; the deer and the squirrels must know. But that one has now been eaten, of course, and the other one nearby that looks just like it might turn out to be the Avenging Angel. On the other hand, a mushroom that's fine for a squirrel might not be fine for us. And maybe that deer skull I found in the woods last week belonged to an overconfident mushroom-loving Bambi. And maybe those same deer and squirrels went on to see terrifying visions of deer and squirrel deities. The woods may be full of hallucinating herbivores.

So I leave wild mushrooms to the experts whose knowledge I admire and almost trust. They seem to know what they're doing. At least they're still alive (but we don't meet the ones who aren't). They remind me a little of Faust, who conjures up six demons, one after the other, confident that he can stay on top of the situation. The day after I saw Busoni's opera *Doktor Faust* I sat down at my desk to write a column, not knowing what the topic would be. Somehow it turned into an essay about mushrooms.

THE DEVIL at the WHEEL

Faust
on the
Freeway

Today Faust drives a Porsche, loaded with all the options: turbo, state-of-the-art stereo (blasting Liszt and Busoni), leather seats, and eternal youth. Cars are the Devil's favorite invention.

They are the vehicles of desire, anarchy, selfishness, and freedom. Trains, by contrast, are pious conveyances. They represent discipline, industriousness, thrift, and co-operation. Trains belong to public authorities and express the deterministic character of the state. Countries where respect for public institutions is strongest, like Switzerland and Japan, are the ones with the best trains. Cars belong to individuals and express the libertarian impulses of their owners. Their libertine desires. Their dreams.

An automobile's metal skin is called a body. Its skin clinics are body shops. Its lithe yet rigid contours evoke an ideal physique. For it serves me, the driver, as a second and superior body, potent and indefatigable. Inside my gleaming carapace, I nestle into an anatomy of vinyl flesh and steel bone that endows me with superhuman power and protection.

My feet no longer trudge but, with a tap to a pedal, launch me into effortless flight. My eyes are magnified as the orbs of headlights. I have no need to shout warnings and threats at those in my way, for the horn's tireless blare is at my fingertips, while my new skin of metal and glass armors me from rebuke.

"You drive like a demon," my passengers complain, as if demons traditionally drove automobiles. It is a Faustian bargain. I renounce my natural connection with society and the biological world, my God-given place with feet on the ground, my ecological conscience. In exchange, I get a semblance of freedom undreamed of before our century except in fables of flying carpets and diabolical broomsticks. I become Faust on the Freeway.

It is a solitary power, for companions, if any, are demoted to the passive state of passengers. The isolation of cars is tailored for couples or family-size groups, but only one person, by custom the man, can be "in the driver's seat." The nuclear family with the man in charge lives on in automotive design. Passengers may offer advice, they may complain, they may ask if we are lost, but real power is beyond their grasp. "Backseat driver" is not a term of respect. Some people never feel so free, so happy, as when driving. However humble their rank on foot, behind the wheel they are kings, philosophers, navigators, demons.

Driving can be hell (where demons come from), but on a good day, with the top down and the wind in one's hair, it is like heaven. Thus Americans celebrate the freedom of the open road. There we feel alive. Our cars give us life. We give them pet names, as if they were dogs or lovers. We speak to them. "Good girl!" some say after a long trip, patting the warm hood; or, on a cold morning, "Come on, you bastard, start!" I congratulated my Volkswagen Rabbit one night on the open road when it reached its one hundred thousandth mile and all the nines on the odometer turned back into zeroes. I decided to invite some other cars to a party, at which toasts of premium oil would be poured to honor the venerable hare.

Some people lovingly wash and polish their cars, yell at strangers who touch them, and house them in special dwellings. Some delight in disassembling and reassembling their machines in greasy rituals of devotion. Others clutter their cars with eccentric collections of personal effects, debris, ornaments, and icons. Their cars become more personal than their homes. Eager to tell the world a favorite politician's name, a religious message, a place where they have been, or a joke, they paste these slogans on their bumpers, not their houses.

Cars express a cult of liberty that verges on anarchy. Drivers are at best strangers to one another, at worst deadly enemies. There are aggressive drivers and defensive drivers, but one who aspires to be a compassionate driver, a charming driver, will not get far on the interstate. In the asphalt jungle, the many thousands of individual decisions add up to a state of disorder that traffic engineers can analyze only through the new science of chaos theory. Freedom becomes fragmentation, and it vanishes as it condenses at random into the hell of gridlock.

Sometimes exhilarating, sometimes maddening, always expensive, this paradoxical ideal of freedom has determined the shape of our landscapes, cities, and thoughts. Its cost is everywhere—from the inner cities to the Arabian desert to the stratosphere, where the greenhouse effect operates. But admit it or not, we love our cars. Nothing separates us more from the way of life of past centuries—and future ones, too.

Driving Lessons

I was driving on the Santa Monica Freeway one day when it began to pour. Los Angelenos have a peculiar relationship with water. It is what runs from a tap or a lawn sprinkler and gurgles in hot tubs. It originates in rivers somewhere inland, to be appropriated by public servants for the sake of green lawns, hot tubs, and swimming pools. At the beach there is a lot more of it, but only to look at or surf on. It is not expected to pour from the sky, and when it does, drivers are confused and helpless. Can they drive in it? They aren't sure. On that rainy day, they pulled over and waited for the end of this dubious miracle: water falling from the heavens.

Then the storm ended, and everyone hurtled back to normal.

Los Angelenos are mellow indoors or on the beach, because (except when interrupted by rain, riots, and earthquakes) they sublimate their aggression behind the wheel. They are skilled at this, having more practice than any other motorists in the world, but woe betide the visitor who loses his nerve in one of their ten-lane labyrinths.

While competing ruthlessly against one another, they defer, surprisingly, to pedestrians, who are a little more common than cloudbursts. It's not like New York, where many people still have the audacity to walk, forcing drivers to take harsh measures to teach them a lesson. When a pedestrian crosses a street in LA, he or she is like a deer crossing a road elsewhere; drivers slow down with feelings of wonder and sympathy for this alien, fragile species. Having won the war against pedestrians long ago, they can afford to be magnanimous.

The fastest drivers in America are in Nevada, where everything is permitted and nothing is worth slowing down to see. In Texas, where there is nothing to see either, except oil wells, the highway police are so fierce that everyone keeps to the speed limit. Forbidden to drive aggressively, Texans find solace in guns. Theirs is the only state where murders outnumber traffic fatalities.

New Jersey drivers have a bad reputation, and the question is often asked: Do they drive that way at home? Yes, they do. No sooner had I crossed the Pennsylvania–New Jersey state line (on the last and most dangerous leg of a cross-country drive) than all the drivers went blooey. Theirs was not the disciplined aggression of the LA freeways nor the systematic terrorism of the streets of Manhattan, but an anarchic, berserk rage. A Mercedes lunged behind me, flashing its lights and honking, swerving from lane to lane in desperation to pass, as the blonde lady behind the wheel grimaced and mouthed imprecations. As it careened by, I saw that it had M.D. plates and three little blond kids in the backseat bobbing up and down in excitement.

Everyone was tailgating and speeding frantically. A police car darted into the thick of the chaos, but nobody slowed down. The traffic was like a school of fish swimming in fast formation; the fish know that all but one of them will make it past the shark. The policeman ticketed that one, a random sacrifice, while the rest continued blithely to run amok.

Cars have been associated with many things—sex, status, freedom—but this was something different, this murderous frenzy. Whatever the cause (the stress of over-population acting on some latent gene? some chemical in the smog?), it was a throwback to a savage state. It was Darwinism on the interstate.

Secret
City

On and off the freeways, Los Angeles has a paradoxical quality of privateness. In contrast to the uninhibited style of its elite—at the wheel, on the screen, at parties, in bed—the city itself is mysterious. It reminds me of towns in the Mediterranean or in Asia, where life goes on behind garden walls and palace facades, hidden from outsiders, sequestered from mayhem.

There is no clear center, no unifying system of public spaces, only the freeways and the beach. The freeways are the sturdy neural connections in the soft tissue of suburban communities that together form the region's character. They are where the middle class is fleetingly to be seen, behind the closed windows of air-conditioned cars, on the way to secret gardens.

Here I feel like H. G. Wells's time traveler, visiting a world where humans have evolved into two species. In *The Time Machine* the subterranean Morlocks do the manual work. The others, who live in the sun, are ethereal and pleasure loving.

In LA, the Morlocks are the people without cars. I glimpse them sometimes, earthbound by the side of the road: homeless camped on the Santa Monica Palisade, Hispanic laborers waiting for buses that seldom appear, aimless crowds around shuttered store fronts. They are not free, cannot travel where and when they please. Only those with cars are free; that is why the roads are called freeways. The mobile class is further subdivided by make and model. As the British place each other by their accents, so in LA you are what you drive, and you tend your car's body as if it were your own.

Those who weary of driving never go anywhere. They wait in their walled gardens for hardier souls to visit them. They spend a lot of time on the phone. Others rate their friends according to how far they have to drive to see them. Those too far are dropped as "GU"—geographically undesirable.

Unlike New York, for instance, where every step delivers a lesson in life's contrasts, Los Angeles is arranged to facilitate oblivion. The space around the freeways can be ignored. It is like outer space. Unspeakable things may be happening in the regions that flash by, where the Morlocks live. But gang wars, riots and racism need not concern the freeway drivers, who never venture beyond the confines of their gardens, cars, offices, and favorite malls. For adventure, they may substitute the virtual space of television and the movies, the city's most famous product. The outside world is the freeway, the TV news and, if they are rich enough, a view of the Pacific.

I swim in the Pacific at Malibu, where the hills over the beach are crowned with modernistic palaces, and I imagine what it would be like to live in one. Here it would be possible to be sincerely unaware that there are troubles in the world. Say I'd made the requisite millions in some innocuous way, like creating a new soap opera concept. Living in Malibu, I might be a genuinely nice person, never having my niceness put to a demanding test. Coddled in luxury and sunshine, mine would be a life of untroubled solipsism, a permanent infancy. I imagine the mansions of Malibu populated by middle-aged babies.

Students of architecture here concern themselves mainly with houses. So do tourists, who peek through locked gates at the outsides of houses. Driving through Beverly Hills, I see a young man sitting at a table near a university campus with a sign offering Star Maps for Sale. For a moment this strikes me as odd. Are there astronomers in these hills? Well, no; these are maps that show the locations of the homes of actors.

Ronald Reagan lives in nearby Bel Air, having returned to his roots—the master of the genial, laid-back exterior, the cue card, and the canned laugh; his inner self unfathomable. Only one detail disturbed him. The street number of his house was 666, which, in the Book of Revelation, is the number of the Beast. He and Nancy had often read that book of the Bible, speculating that the day of judgment would soon dawn, but he did not like to be numbered as the Beast. He did not like living at the Devil's address. So he changed the number to 668.

The houses I visit are charming: flimsily constructed but full of light and organized around interior gardens which, like Roman atria, give a feeling of seclusion that belies their tiny size and the proximity of streets and neighbors.

Of the people I meet, only one actually grew up in Los Angeles. Many are exiled New Yorkers. Two speak fervently of their new life in LA as they show me their garden, hot tub, and painting studio. The wife has lost the haggard look that marked her when last seen, a year ago in a dark apartment in New York. The circles under her eyes are gone. She no longer complains. She seems happy.

But others, who have lived here longer, speak of the

smog, the real estate prices, and a more fearsome specter—savage police and black rage.

The seductive quality of life in the hidden gardens of Los Angeles masks a premonition of catastrophe. I find myself looking at the city as at something to be enjoyed while it lasts. There are, I think, more apocalyptic science fiction novels and movies set here than in any other city. How appropriate that J. Paul Getty, when he built the richest museum in the world in Malibu (open only to those arriving by car), modeled it after a villa in Pompeii.

Geology is destiny. I see banners in Santa Monica announcing Earthquake Awareness Week and Water Conservation Month. The city is waiting for an earthquake. Its lushness thrives on scarce water filched from the countryside hundreds of miles inland. Its atmosphere is in peril. Its Morlocks are insurgent. Its most famous citizen lives at number 666, even if he pretends it is 668. Meanwhile, it's beguiling.

Virtual City

After driving around Los Angeles for several days, try-ing to make sense of the place, I visit Disneyland and find the town center I've been looking for. Disneyland is to Los Angeles what the Acropolis is to Athens. Where I expected a tacky amusement park, I find a prodigy of architectural myth making, of brilliantly organized show-manship, of whimsical glory. The place is thronged with Japanese tourists, agog at what America still does best.

Disneyland is movie making translated into building and ritual. It is an evolving tradition. Walt Disney's sce-nario is still being worked out today by his apostles, in-cluding the director George Lucas, who designed two of the newest rides in Tomorrowland around themes from *Star Wars*.

It is a miniature city with a quarter for each of var-ious compartments of the American psyche: childhood fantasy, adventure, the frontier, Main Street, the ideal city (New Orleans), trains, freeways, and space travel. Evil is represented only on thrill rides that pass in darkness through a town sacked by lifelike mechanical pirates and through a haunted house where ghosts are given eerie, translucent form by the most up-to-date holographic techniques.

The pirates are all we see of greed, war, or slavery.

The ghosts are all we see of death. There is a comical face to the pirates and ghosts, which reassures. There is humor, too, in nature, among the singing bears, and in the future, which holds nothing more dire than a space-suited Michael Jackson in 3-D. The Devil does not show his real face in Disneyland.

Money is not a problem there; the ticket one buys at the gate is good for all rides. For food and souvenirs, one has the option of spending Disney dollars—convertible from real ones, one for one, at the gate—which bear a portrait of Mickey Mouse instead of George Washington.

There is a police force but you never see it; the guards are disguised as cartoon characters. Main Street includes the most nostalgic features of small-town life, impeccably idealized—a general store, a soda fountain, a bandstand, and so on—but nothing suggesting the wrong side of the tracks. There is no other side of the tracks, for the railroad circles along the edge of Disneyland. There is no church on Main Street. Wise Mr. Disney knew his limits. God—like sex, death, and politics—is beyond the scope of his project.

During the turbulent sixties, Disneyland denied admittance to any male with long hair, just as its culture conveniently skips that era. The fifties, a once-upon-a-time to the children there today and the nostalgic past for their parents, are now part of the theme. Along with Snow White and Goofy, Disney employees in the streets impersonate clean fifties teenagers, Pat Boone clones.

A nighttime concert features the Ventures, a long-lived band (George Bush's favorite, and mine too when I was 12) that plays rock and roll without the words. Detroit chariots from the fifties are parked in the town squares, shiny and glittering; fresh from the factory, they seem (or from a car wash in the fountain of youth). Five of them are filled almost to the roof with fifties artifacts—Hula-Hoops, Frisbees, yo-yos, Slinkys, and paddle balls—for a contest in which whoever guesses how many there are has a chance to win the car.

Coveting a red and white Corvette full of yo-yos, I spend a few minutes estimating the interior volume of the car and the volume of a yo-yo, a process by which long division plus inspired guesswork yields a figure of 2,189. I fill out my contest ticket and put it in the box by the Corvette. For a week, until somebody else wins the car, I dream a dream of the mythical fifties.

Walt Disney knew what he was doing when he set out to build a city that gave form to the innocence in the American character. The tourists seem, without exception (myself included), to have shed their cares for the day. No one complains about the crowds or the lines. The people who run Disneyland mean what they say when they bill it as "the happiest place on earth."

But after midnight the place is empty. Everyone has vanished, like Cinderella. This happiest place, this home-town of the mind, is a place where nobody lives.

Dallas

Nobody lives, either, in downtown Dallas. I have always thought of Dallas as the unhappiest place, a town with bad karma. The year I was in seventh grade, the headmaster wandered into the carpentry shop one November day, a transistor radio to his ear, and told us Kennedy had been shot. In Dallas. Recently I saw *The Thin Blue Line*, a documentary about an innocent man who was sentenced to death there in a murder frame-up. Dallas heroes are the cowboy, the oilman, and H. Ross Perot. But it's on my route; I've been on the road a week, heading for Arizona and California. I figure I'll spend the night in Dallas and see if I was wrong.

After Nashville and Memphis, two decayed cities trying for a rebound, Dallas is different. It hasn't had time to decay. Downtown is a collection of enormous, gleaming, postmodern office towers, with no people in the streets after working hours.

It's eerie and sad to walk these hot glass canyons, deserted at only 7 P.M. It is like a dream or a science fiction movie; the shiny city stretches on forever, but I am alone because the inhabitants have fled. With relief I discover life in the so-called historic district (historic in Dallas being anything built before 1950), or West End, which consists of several dozen brick buildings renovated as trendy shops, bars, and restaurants.

The largest, a typical eighties-style redevelopment, contains a five-story emporium where the shops sell delicacies (including many varieties of chili powder), compact disks (but not books), electronic gadgets, celebrity autographs, Dallas T-shirts, ecological toys, and implements designed for left-handed people. There is also a peculiar museum of the Kennedy assassination, devoted to the promulgation of conspiracy theories.

The plaza outside, and the streets leading to it, are jammed with young people, a couple of thousand of them, waiting for a free outdoor concert by the rock band Blood, Sweat and Tears. I have a superb steak at a nearby restaurant. Dallas, I decide, isn't so bad. Later I hear a bit of the concert (not realizing yet how apt the band's name is to the locale) and pick my way through beer-drinking rock fans, back in the direction of my hotel, an elegant old place, built in 1912 by a beer tycoon, where a pianist plays Chopin waltzes in the lobby.

I notice that the crowded "historic district" is surrounded by crowded parking lots. All those people drove here. Nobody lives here. The West End is less an example of successful urban renewal than a case of a former city center retrofitted as a mall. It is a counterfeit downtown.

Between the parking lots and my hotel is another barren commercial zone. It's around 10. I pass some panhandlers, some homeless people sitting on benches, dwarfed by the glittering skyscrapers above them, a few souls waiting forlornly for a bus, and some streets with no people or cars in sight at all. I look around and see two men behind me, one on each side of the street. Are they following me?

I walk a little faster. I won't run. After all, I'm a New

Yorker. All my life I've walked the maligned streets of Gotham at all hours with never any trouble. The hotel is only a block away. As a tall, male liberal, I'm damned if I'll accede to urban prejudice, overreacting to the proximity of two men who happen to be black.

A bus goes by on the avenue before me. One of the men shouts, "There's the bus! Run for it!" That turns out to be their standard operating procedure.

I hear their running footsteps and assume they are racing to catch the bus until—wham!—the guy behind me delivers a terrific blow to my head, then another, and another, while his companion across the street darts over and pins my arms. The first one keeps pounding my head. (With what? A cosh, a two-by-four, his fists? Beats me. He stays behind me and I never see what hits me.) Neither says a word. I never get a good look at them. They stay behind me the whole time. They're pros.

For a few seconds, as the first man bangs away, all I feel is stunned amazement. Then I begin struggling in the other man's grip, and yelling, as if there were anyone else to hear.

Suddenly they're gone, leaving me reeling, bleeding from a gash over my right eye, and (as I soon discover) without my wallet. I stagger down the street. A lone passerby stares at me in alarm and hurries on his way. I come to a restaurant, a greasy spoon called Subway, where the cook is just closing up. He looks at me without surprise, gives me a wad of napkins for the bleeding, and calls the police.

The cops are not friendly. They're annoyed because I can't describe the assailants. "But they were black, weren't they?" one asks. "At least you know that?" An emergency medical van pulls up. The men inside are cheerful. One recognizes me from the Blood, Sweat and Tears concert, where the van was stationed in case the fans rioted. They bandage my head. They say that probably my nose is broken and maybe I have a concussion. They give me the name of a hospital. But they can't drive me there, they say. They have to go straight back to the concert. I should take a taxi. Walletless, I say I'll have to go back to the hotel and cash a traveler's check. Not a good idea, the man says earnestly; not safe to walk there at night; too bad it's against the rules for them to drive me the block to the hotel. None of this makes sense—especially their concern that I might be assaulted all over again. Any muggers with eyes in their heads will see I've already met their colleagues. The two urge me to be careful and drive off in a U-turn back to the concert.

The hotel receptionist doesn't seem a bit surprised when I walk in bandaged and bloody. I take a cab to the emergency room, where I wait an hour because two men with bullet wounds have triage priority. One has shot himself in the leg by mistake. He'd been about to drive somewhere in his pickup truck, and while opening the door put his gun on the roof. The gun fell on the ground and went off. He's complaining loudly because he's in pain and isn't being treated first, either. The nurse tells him to stop feeling sorry for himself. "Look there," she says, as another man is wheeled by on a gurney, his face covered with bandages. "He wasn't shot by no mistake, and not in the leg either."

Two other men walk in. The younger tells the nurse he's bringing his uncle to see a doctor. The uncle doesn't speak English. They've driven from Mexico, been on the road 11 hours, the nephew says.

"What's the matter with your uncle?" she asks.

"He has the hiccups."

"And how long has he been hiccuping?"

"Eight years."

The nurses in surreal Dallas are sweet to me. They can't believe I've come all the way from New York to be mugged in their city. They x-ray my head from eight different angles and find nothing broken. The doctor who stitches me up says, "No Dallasite ever goes downtown at night without his gun."

Dallas, I decide, has some nice people living in it after all. It's not their fault the city is accursed. And Dallas has a fine hospital, which it surely needs. It has good steak restaurants. A nifty art museum. A fairly good newspaper. The front-page feature in the next morning's Dallas *Times Herald* is an interview with Randall Dale Adams, the frame-up victim, who is living with his mother in Ohio and trying to figure out what to do with his life now that *The Thin Blue Line* has brought about his exoneration. He'll never go back to Dallas, either.

The experience of reality banging me on the head leaves me astonished, then relieved. There's been no time in between for fear. It's disagreeable but quickly done with; an interruption, not an ending. I feel oddly stronger: here's a test I had often heard about, wondered about, and assumed I would never encounter; now I have, and it wasn't so bad. I finish the night with nine stitches, an egg-size bump on the back of my head, a number of other bumps and welts, a black eye (purple actually), and the loss of an old wallet containing a few dollars and credit cards. I need new glasses, too. But nothing else is broken. The pain wasn't much worse than a serious visit to the dentist. I'm lucky. I could be that guy in the hospital with a bullet in his head.

I'm angry too, but it's hard to focus anger on two men I can't visualize. Sure I'd like the bastards jailed, but there's no hope of that, when I can't tell the police anything but what color they are. I can't be like the pope, who forgave his would-be assassin, but nor will I fit the cliché that says a conservative is a liberal who's just been mugged. I'm not about to pack a pistol or vote Republican. I'm glad, though, to get back in my car ("Hope you enjoyed your stay," says the garage attendant) and see the last of Dallas.

No Smoking
in the
Parthenon

Lucky the place that boasts a monument that expresses an authentic identity: Moscow's St. Basil's, New York's Empire State Building, Cairo's pyramids. Other communities, less favored by the historical and architectural muses, sometimes jump to the conclusion that, if only they too had some grand emblem, something like an Eiffel Tower or a Golden Gate Bridge, some grand simulacrum of urban character—then civic pride would rebound, tourists would come, and economic woes would disappear.

So they raise money and build something big. The would-be monument symbolizes something or other to do with its city's name or desired image. Usually, however, it ends up towering in forlorn isolation above the urban decay it was intended to reverse, waiting for tourists who never do arrive.

There can be an element of grandeur in their absurdity. One approaches them with incredulous wonder, thinking: This really exists. It's not just a story in a newspaper. They actually went and spent lots of money and did this.

Look on my works, ye mighty, and do a double take.

Such were my thoughts when I first saw the St. Louis Arch—and again when, in the course of my cross-country drive (two days before Dallas), I viewed the Nashville Parthenon and the Memphis Pyramid.

Yes, Tennessee has both a full-scale replica of the Parthenon and a 300-foot-high pyramid. The latter, sheathed in stainless steel, gleams beside the Mississippi like something that might have landed in a Spielberg movie. It's so bright in the midsummer sun that it's painful to look at.

The pyramid had been scheduled to open for tourists in 1991, shortly before I saw it. It was to contain a country music auditorium and an amusement park with horror rides (Egyptian gods, mummies, and so forth). A triangular elevator was to convey tourists diagonally upward along a notch in the pyramid's edge to an observation room in its apex.

But apparently the developer who was building it ran out of the money that he'd talked the city into raising for him. So the pyramid gleamed unfinished on a barren construction site flanked by expressways and urban blight.

The idea propounded by the developer and his friends in city government went something like this: Memphis is the name of an old city in Egypt. Egypt has pyramids. Tourists go to Egypt to see pyramids. Therefore, build a pyramid in the new Memphis and tourists will come here too.

The symbolism was perhaps misguided, aiming to revitalize a moribund city center by reproducing the form of an ancient tomb. Also, it was a mistake to sheath it in shiny steel. Not only can't you look at it without hurting your eyes, but you can't get too close without getting cooked; the side facing the sun, acting as a giant solar reflector, produces a double heat wave in the streets nearby. This pyramid seems to be accursed even without a mummy to do the cursing.

The St. Louis Arch is equally ambiguous in its symbolism. It represents the city's idea of itself as the Gateway to the West. But it is in the nature of open gateways that one passes through them without stopping. And this one, unlike the triumphal arches of Rome or Paris, or the arch in New York's Washington Square, is barren of all ornament. It is a colossal, half-buried zero, a Brobdingnagian croquet wicket. It has no function, no connection to the urban fabric, no charm.

Nashville's Parthenon, on the other hand, is charming in a quirky way, like a piece of folk art. The city, which boosters used to call the Athens of the South, built the temple for a centennial exposition back in 1897 and has been taking loving care of it ever since, renovating it in 1931 and 1988 and recently furnishing its interior hall, called the Naos, with a 42-foot-tall statue of Athena.

The building's proportions duplicate those of the original, but otherwise the new Athenians went their own way. Their Parthenon stands on flat ground, in a park. It's built of sandstone, not marble. It boasts the world's largest bronze doors (seven and a half tons), cast by the General Bronze Corporation of Long Island City.

The city's art museum is inside, one flight down from the Naos. This is a Parthenon with electric lighting, restrooms, and signs that say No Smoking in the Parthenon. Outside, kids play Frisbee on the lawn beneath the sandstone friezes.

The Athena statue, which a Nashville artist spent eight years constructing, isn't made of marble either. In his speculative recreation of the lost Phidias original, the sculptor used "a compound of gypsum cement and chopped fiberglass bonded onto a structural steel framework."

The effect of this gypsum goddess, spotlighted between rows of reddish pillars, isn't particularly Greek. It has a definite character all its own—somewhere between Disneyland and the Statue of Liberty. It is pop, like Nashville's better-known attraction, Opryland, or Memphis's Graceland—Elvis's pop Monticello.

There were tourists in Memphis, all right, who came from as far away as Liverpool and Tokyo, but they were there to visit the shrine of Elvis. None of them could have cared less about a steel pyramid.

Unless . . . now here's an idea for the Memphis tourism commission. Sell the bankrupt pyramid to the Presley estate. Put the King's mortal remains inside. Let them be viewed there in a glass case in a royal burial chamber. Then tourists will flock to these steel portals, agog at the mummy of Elvis I (and finally believe he's truly dead).

Hey
Mr. Rockefeller

Driving home to New York, I stopped for lunch one day in Reno. I thought that a city built for games might be fun. It wasn't. Greed, not games, was the operative principle there, and greed is the grimmest of vices. Also the most durable. Long after lust, gluttony, and the other passions that money can feed have withered away, the lure of money in the abstract beckons dourly on.

I wandered into a casino, a hall vast as an airplane hangar but windowless and stuffy. The place was crammed wall to wall with slot machines. They whirred, jangled, and flashed with infernal vulgarity.

At each machine sat a cheerless and usually elderly person, bent and intent, mechanically stuffing it with coins or dollar tokens with one hand, pulling its lever with the other. They toiled ceaselessly, expressionlessly, like zombies—showing, whether they won or lost, the same lack of joy or any other human attribute except concentration. If one of these wizened addicts hit the jackpot, the prize money went straight back into the machine. They won in order to bet their winnings on winning again. This dream alone, going round and round on itself, fired their withered synapses.

The old men tended to look like Ivan Boesky, the legendary financier who proclaimed, "Greed is all right."

When Boesky went to jail for insider trading, he shed his natty suits and confident demeanor and became unkempt and weird, like the slot machine addicts, and like Howard Hughes, who in his declining years shunned all human contact and lurked like a spider in his Las Vegas penthouse, living only for the idea of spinning money into more money.

"Hey Mr. Rockefeller, are you having fun?" Bette Midler asked in a song in which she imagined telephoning the billionaire with this interesting question.

Nelson Rockefeller, I think, would have truthfully answered yes, for he was not the Rockefeller who made the money, but the grandson who spent it on his lusty games of politics and art collecting. He even died having fun, according to the conclusion popularly drawn from the circumstances of his demise in a young lady's apartment.

But his grandfather, the founder of the dynasty, did not have fun. Photographs show him grim as a mummy. Ivan Boesky in his heyday was not having fun. In photos he looks alone and sad. So does his accomplice and mentor Michael Milken, who made more money in a shorter time than perhaps anyone in history, but never did anything else with his time.

The old people at the slot machines in Reno were not having fun. Nevada is not fun. The film *Bugsy* lied when it cast Warren Beatty as the gangster and pretended that his scheme of developing the desert with a garish pavilion where people could throw their money away was a kind of transcendent dream.

The part of Nevada I drove through struck me as a wasteland where nobody in his right mind would live except out of abstract greed. So did parts of Texas I traversed after Dallas, where there was practically nothing to see except those greed-driven engines, the oil wells pioneered by the Rockefeller patriarch.

People went to Nevada to mine the grim, arid wastes for gold, uranium, and other toxic things. Still discontent, they put their heads together with people like Bugsy to think of some other, more potent kind of greed to further their addiction, to bring in more addicts—and they hit on the idea of gambling.

A case was made during the Reagan years that greed is really all right, as Boesky said—a stimulus for the economy. Its legacy in the Bush years, including the disgrace of people like Boesky and Milken, argued otherwise. Either way, it's the vice of the living dead. Only the Devil laughs in Reno.

RIDING the BOMB

The Lemon
That
Exploded

My first car was a little white Porsche. One day it broke down in the parking lot of Long Island's first (and last) nuclear plant. Both were lemons. The Long Island Lighting Company spent $5 billion and 18 years building the plant, which was called Shoreham, and then sold it for $1 to New York State, which is taking it apart again.

The company's officials were sad about that. The plant was a big part of their lives. They used to speak of it with an air of defensive but sincere enthusiasm—as a man speaks of a powerful new sports car that cost too much and doesn't work right and makes his wife nervous, but which he's been dreaming about for a long time and is now more determined than ever to get on the road, to feel its power at last and show everyone what a splendid machine it really is.

They dreamed of building several more like it. But by the time they finished it, years behind schedule, having spent the company almost into bankruptcy, the voting public was frightened. Antinuclear protests, journalistic exposés, and government investigations indicated that the company was way over its head in an unfamiliar and dangerous technology, had lost control of the project, and had sited it in a spot from which Long Island's geography and congested highways would make evacuation impossible.

A couple of politicians who frankly supported Shore-ham were voted out, and the others quickly vied to outdo each other in proclamations of antinuclear zeal. Privately, some of them assured company officials that they had to say these things to get elected, and that they expected the plant to open anyway. They expected other politicians higher up in the hierarchy to overrule them and make sure it opened. But when all the politicians right up to the governor embraced the antinuclear movement as an apple-pie issue, no one was left to take the responsibility, and it never did open.

But about my first car. It was a little white Porsche, model 914, as lovely as it was temperamental. As a boy I'd dreamed of driving an Austin-Healey, an MGB, or a Tri-umph Spitfire, but as a 21-year-old with a new job as a local newspaper reporter, able at last to afford a Spitfire, I sat in one for the first time and found that my legs were way too long to fit. So I bought a Porsche 914, which by virtue of its engine's placement behind the driver's seat (a fateful detail) had plenty of leg room.

Now long discontinued, with good reason, the 914 was a cross between a Volkswagen and a real Porsche: a two-seater with a bargain price that was soon canceled out by the costs of towing, repairs, and speeding tickets. It ran like the wind when it ran, which depended on the weather. On any day that was particularly cold, hot, or rainy, it would not start at all, and in our five years together it stranded me in many cold, hot, wet, and gener-ally inconvenient places, such as the Long Island Express-way, the middle of New Jersey, and the parking lot of the Shoreham plant.

It was cool in the depths of the plant that June day in 1977, as company executives proudly led a group of us reporters, sporting hardhats, through the unfinished concrete labyrinth to the innermost sanctum of the reactor. The place reminded me of the Egyptian pyramid in which, some years before, with similar feelings of awe and claustrophobia, I had wriggled up a long, dark tunnel to the burial chamber. Shoreham, however, was full of construction workers who seemed to be milling about and giving us furtive looks. I would remember these looks later when press reports alleged that those workers had often whiled away their days sleeping, stealing equipment, smoking pot, and (when they were actually working) making up the wiring and plumbing pretty much as they went along.

Outside, meanwhile, the day had grown hot as the Sahara, and when it came time to leave, my little Porsche proved stubborn as a camel in its insolent, familiar refusal to start. I was rescued by the Long Island Lighting Company's vice president for public affairs and three members of his staff. They pushed. I steered. Laboriously we rolled across the parking lot until I slipped the engine into gear; it roared to life, the PR people laughed and waved, and I sped home, the only beneficiary of energy produced at Shoreham.

The Porsche came to a sad end that August, when its engine caught fire on a dirt road in Montauk, near the tip of Long Island. I was noticing a strong smell of gas. Then my girlfriend, driving her trusty Volkswagen behind me, started beeping her horn. I looked in the rearview mirror and saw flaming puddles of gas in the road. I jumped out with the fire extinguisher I carried in the car and sprayed it into the engine, but the flames only grew. As I retreated to a prudent distance, the car began to blaze like a great blowtorch, with a steady rage, fed by the gas that continued to flow from the tank, down the ruptured fuel line, to the engine. One by one the tires overcooked and exploded with a boom. A column of thick black smoke mounted into the still sky, looking like a scene from a war movie. A plane approaching the nearby airport circled around the plume. Apparently the pilot radioed the airport controller, who called the fire department. I heard distant sirens. By the time the fire truck arrived, the magnesium engine block had ignited. It burned with an intense heat that water wouldn't snuff. Finally, the fire fighters got out shovels and buried it in sand.

They were laughing, but I didn't see anything funny. The car had vexed me often, even to cries of frustration, and had endangered my life more than once, as when it had spun like a pinwheel on a suddenly ice-sheeted highway while I shivered with fear and cold (the heater didn't work). But even so, I grieved to see it now, a blackened hulk. Everything inside was incinerated, including a copy of a Faulkner novel I'd been meaning to read, *Light in August*. When the fire trucks backed away a police car appeared, and I recognized the officer in sunglasses who regarded me expressionlessly. I'd written some articles about a scandal in which two policemen had burglarized a local fish store and taken a box of shrimp back to headquarters as a treat for themselves and their colleagues on the midnight shift. This policeman was one of those who had eaten the shrimp. There was a sardonic note in his voice as he called across the wreckage: "How're you doing today, Mr. Schaffner?"

My insurance company, guided by an appraisal book whose authors didn't know the 1972 Porsche 914 was a lemon, paid me almost as much as it had cost new: enough to buy the no-nonsense VW Rabbit that would serve me faithfully for nine years.

Meanwhile, the Porsche company mailed me a recall notice, warning of a design flaw that could cause engine fires. The engine was just behind the driver's seat, and its grille was placed flat across the rear hood, with a metal trough underneath to catch rainwater, which, however, would overflow in a downpour. A fire, the letter explained, might happen like this: the overflowing rainwater could drip onto the battery, where it could pick up acid and then drip further, onto the nearby gas line, in which, over a period of years, the acid rain might eat a hole, causing gas to spurt out suddenly and possibly ignite. It was one of those freak chains of cause and effect that engineers (automotive or nuclear) often can't anticipate and that one day lead to catastrophe. Now the people at Porsche, alerted by a spate of fires, were recalling 914s all over the country to be refitted with waterproof battery covers and acid-resistant fuel lines. They were three weeks late for me.

Eight years later, I returned to Shoreham for another press tour of the finally completed nuclear plant. The company officials were still hoping to start it up, insisting and convincing themselves that there was nothing the matter with it, that it was the best and safest nuclear plant in the world.

The vice president for public affairs was still there, friendly as ever. He wanted to know if I was still driving the little sports car he and his staff had push-started. I told him it had burned up. Then I tried to make a joke. "It was kind of like Shoreham," I told him. "It never started when I wanted it to, and finally it had a meltdown." He didn't laugh.

Atomic Fireballs

When I was a kid, F. A. O. Schwarz sold a toy nuclear power plant. I played with models of bombers and submarines and a Corgi toy Pershing missile. I sucked on a candy called Atomic Fireballs. These things were part of a ritual of placation. Mine was the atomic generation.

We were the first children ever to grow up knowing that at any moment all of us, everywhere, could suddenly be dead. Not just dead as in "Bang bang, cowboy, you're dead!" Or dead like my cat Henry and my Uncle Melvin and other old folks who occasionally vanished discreetly from life, one by one, with a dignified church ritual perhaps marking their departure. But dead all at the same time, in a blinding flash and a million-degree fireball, leaving nothing behind but a melted belt buckle or eyeglass frame, or a silhouette outlined by the scorching blast on a fragment of wall standing alone in a wasteland of wreckage, like the reverse shadow I remembered from a Hiroshima documentary, left by someone walking down the street at the instant the bomb went off.

It was a knowledge beyond the knowledge of evil. If this were the Devil's work, he could not have realized the implications, for he needs a world full of living people in which to pursue his aims. It was a blind lunacy beyond evil that shadowed the lives of good people and wicked people alike.

We knew this even as children. I would dream about bombers and missiles in the sky over New York. It was necessary to placate the nightmares, to contain them, to put the genie back in the bottle over and over again. Adults, wittingly or not, provided the means to trivialize the specter, or to understand it in a technical sense—that masculine sense in which to understand how something works is to make it less fearsome. Hence the toys, the candy, the science fiction stories about nuclear survivors and mutants, the brochures and magazine articles about blast zones and fallout shelters.

But the dread would not go away. It came back worse than ever with the Cuban missile crisis. My strongest memory of those days is the expression on a teacher's face as he watched us children playing in the schoolyard during recess.

We knew what was up. We read the headlines. We saw the serious faces on the television news, and the aerial photos of missile bases. A couple of teachers came to school with transistor radios, which they held to their ears between classes, intent on the latest bulletins. Normally these dignified men lived in a different world from the one of transistor radios. Something had to be very wrong.

But life went on. There were classes and homework and horsing around at recess. A friend and I were shoving and insulting each other, as on any normal day, when I looked over and met the teacher's gaze, his look of sad, terrible knowledge.

I can guess what he must have been thinking: that we might have only a few days or hours to live; that he had lived the best part of his life already, while we 11-year-olds ought to have ours ahead of us; that he knew this and believed that we did not. Perhaps there was also guilt in his expression, at being part of a generation that was so close to betraying its children.

The crisis passed; life went on. Walking home from the bus stop after school one day, I discovered a Civil Defense office newly opened in a storefront on Lexington Avenue. Behind the display window was a life-size mock-up of a fallout shelter, inhabited by a family of dummies, with cans of soup, cans of water, flashlights, and the other paraphernalia of postnuclear life.

I went in and picked up some pamphlets. They described how to build a shelter and what to do when the bomb went off. I checked out my family's basement for a likely site, and explained to my father why we needed one. He retorted that the idea was madness.

I thought I was the realist in that argument, but my father believed such a concept of survival was meaningless. There were many who did not agree. Nelson Rockefeller had a shelter drilled into the bedrock 100 feet under his town house on West 54th Street, with an elevator in which he planned to descend as the bombs fell, later to emerge amid the radioactive rubble and resume his place in society.

At 11 or 12, I could tell you the difference between an atom bomb, a hydrogen bomb, and a "dirty" cobalt bomb; such things were explained in the popular science magazines I read, and in the Civil Defense pamphlets, with their drawings of concentric circles showing the distances from ground zero within which everything would be vaporized, blasted, burned, or merely irradiated. It was an abstract kind of knowledge. I did not recognize its madness. Fear was pushed into the background, to surface only in my nightmares, or in movies about radiation-spawned monsters from the deep.

The nuclear toys were both titillating and reassuring: a make-believe mastery, a plastic pornography of death that rendered it seemingly harmless and miniature. My friends and I assembled models of missiles, submarines, and bombers. F. A. O. Schwarz sold the toy nuclear plant. Atomic Fireballs were bright red, spicy cinnamon balls, with a picture of a mushroom cloud in red on the yellow box.

My model of a Polaris missile sub was one of the Aurora company's most popular. The KGB bought one; it was easier than stealing a blueprint. (Nervous agent in toy store; parcel smuggled to USSR in diplomatic pouch; box solemnly opened in Moscow to reveal hundreds of tiny grey plastic parts; much head-scratching as KGB experts try to figure out instructions; coded telegram to New York: "Send glue.")

It was a notoriously accurate model. Congress demanded to know how such vital national secrets had fallen into the hands of the toy company. It didn't bother them that American youngsters were amusing themselves with this symbol of doom. They just didn't want Soviet grown-ups to have it.

It was a strange culture of denial that transmuted death into toys, candy, and cheerful tableaux of nuclear families in fallout shelters. The people who worked in the Civil Defense office must have known, if they stopped to think for a minute, that their advice was preposterous in New York City. The people who thought up the idea of telling schoolchildren to take cover under their desks in a nuclear attack, as I remember being taught to do in first grade, must have known that this was an empty ritual.

Everyone knew it; few could contemplate it for more than a moment, the occasional stab of anxiety, soon pushed out of mind by the press of daily life. The Cuban missile crisis was the exception. That one time death passed near, and everyone knew it. For those 13 days, it could no longer be denied or trivialized. A connection was made between imagery and experience: between the specter of "the button" that could unleash fiery doom, and the weary faces of the men with their fingers on that button, the aerial photos that brought them to the brink, and the news footage of American warships intercepting Soviet freighters with ominous crates on their decks. The same terrible knowledge I remember on my teacher's face hit home in many places, even in the White House and the Kremlin.

Years later I read Robert Kennedy's memoir of the crisis, in which he described his brother John's frame of mind in those days: "The thought that disturbed him the most, and that made the prospect of war much more fearful than it would otherwise have been, was the specter of the death of the children of this country and all the world—the young people who had no role, who had no say, who knew nothing even of the confrontation [although many of us did have a sense of it], but whose lives would be snuffed out like everyone else's."

And I read the memoirs of Nikita Khrushchev, who recalled the Kremlin leaders' "anxiety, which was intense," while their American counterparts, in his opinion, "were no less scared than we were of atomic war. We hadn't had time to deliver all our shipments to Cuba, but we had installed enough missiles already to destroy New York, Chicago, and the other huge industrial cities, not to mention a little village like Washington. I don't think

America had ever faced such a real threat of destruction as at that moment."

If we are farther from the brink today, after 30 years of inching erratically back, one reason is that we once stepped so close, looked over, and realized truly where we were. Children today have an uncertain future in many ways; many will die or suffer from AIDS, poverty, war, ecological disaster, and other new calamities; but they are also lucky. Their parents survived those 13 days in 1962 to bring them into life, and probably will never have to look at them with the depth of pity and sorrow, the totality of horror, that I remember in the face of that teacher as he watched us at our games.

Gladiators
and
Astronauts

The Romans had gladiators to inure the populace to the spectacle of combat and to provide young men with a rite of passage that trained them for war. Americans have football.

The football is a bomb. Take the nose of an artillery shell, double it back on itself, and you have a football, a warhead that can be fired in either direction. There is a movie called *The Mouse That Roared* about a tiny country that joined the big league with a weapon even more potent than an H-bomb: the Q-bomb. It looked like a football.

Football is played by warriors—helmeted, uniformed, numbered—who huddle in a council of military strategy and decide how to deliver their bomb to the enemy's heartland. They encounter a strategic defense. Ronald Reagan never forgot his movie role as a star football player. His Strategic Defense Initiative was a dream of football in outer space.

Penetration of the goal brings despair to the enemy ranks and rejoicing to the invaders and their fans in the bleachers, the civilian population, who utter fierce exhortations. I attended a boarding school whose traditional rival on the football field wore green. "What do we eat? Green meat!" we shouted in the stands. The night before the big game, at a pep rally around a bonfire, a green-uniformed effigy was burned at the stake. The rite, with its cannibalistic chant, harked back to the prehistory of war, when slain foes were ceremonially roasted and eaten. At football games, a military band joins in the exhortation, accompanied by the gyrations of cheerleaders, Valkyries beckoning those who excel in battle, promising themselves to the victors.

Football is the most overt of games that symbolize war. Those less brawny, more brainy, and equally aggressive play chess, whose murderous strategies culminate in a symbolic castration. This happens when the tallest and most important but most vulnerable chess piece, the king, is caught in a pincer movement (by a queen and a bishop, say), and the loser acknowledges checkmate by knocking the piece from its upright position, severing it from the board.

Among other sports, the marathon is named after a battle. Race horses are descended from cavalry. The javelin, the shot, the archer's arrow, and the marksman's bullet were invented as weapons. The target shooter aims for an eye that is euphemistically attributed to a bull. The bowling alley is an artillery range where cannonballs "strike" down enemy ranks.

Baseball is different. It enjoys a more spiritual mystique. In the film *Field of Dreams,* it represents an occult quest, and the hero learns in a vision that constructing a ball field will bring him salvation. There is a book called *The Physics of Baseball.* Nobody cares about the physics of football (only the physiques). Celebrity watchers in my town look forward to a trendy summer event known as the Artists-Writers Softball Game. Football has no such cachet.

In football, soccer, basketball, and the like, the aggressor aims to penetrate a particular confined space, a goal or basket. In baseball, as in tennis, the idea is the reverse: to hit the ball away from confinement, to let it fly free of interception by the opponent's mitt or racket.

Freedom is the theme of baseball as war is of football. The player, alone and unarmored on home plate, with the entire opposing team arrayed against him, wants to hit the ball right out of the field. When the ball flies, he can run. If he hits it so well that the adversary fails in all attempts at timely interception, he is free to run home.

Baseball is an ideal that transcends the moral failings of its participants (boorish fans, greedy or druggy stars). It is less a battle than a ballet. It expresses a positive side of the American character: the longing to surpass limits, to excel as an individual against the group, to run free, to come home. That is why it is, along with jazz and the movies, America's most popular cultural export. When democracy came to Japan, so did baseball. Today it is catching on in Russia.

I'll go even farther out (into left field) and suggest a kinship between the baseball player and the astronaut, between the urge to hit a ball out of the park and to send a craft into free orbit. Someday, when American and Russian co-spacefarers play the first ball game on Mars, it will be baseball, not football.

A Dream
of
Pluto

A rocket almost as big as Yankee Stadium was the dream of a physicist who designed nuclear weapons and who sought to redeem his hellish creations by using them to power a spaceship. "Saturn by 1970" was the slogan of his project, which was called Orion. A team of scientists worked enthusiastically on the Orion design until 1963, when the U.S. government cut off funding because the rocket's explosions would have violated the nuclear test ban treaty.

The engine would have resembled a vast upside-down bowl, with a hole in the middle from which the bombs, 2,000 of them, were to be ejected one at a time, one per second, their explosive force focused downward by the ship's concave underside. With so much power, there was no need to stint on the ship's mass. This space-ship would have been a leviathan, and very fast, with plenty of room for passengers and whatever they wanted to take along—even a piano.

The physicist, Theodore Taylor, planned to be on board when the ship made its maiden tour of the solar system. He told the writer John McPhee, who profiled him in the book *The Curve of Binding Energy*, "I dreamed of looking out a porthole at the rings of Saturn, some-times the moons of Jupiter. . . . The remotest place I expected to see was Pluto, where the sun is a pale disc and there is deep twilight at noon. Cold, cold, cold. But still a world."

I thought of this scientist's dream while watching Voyager's images of Neptune, broadcast from the farthest-yet reaches of space in the summer of 1989. Suppose a human being and not a robot had been out there beholding those sights. Knowing that, we would have experienced a different, even more exciting event: the difference between a marvel and a drama.

Who now remembers the photos of the moon taken by the unmanned Surveyor probes, compared with the manned landings? Who would send an automated TV camera to a mountain peak, if he were able to climb it himself?

I'm not suggesting we send a crew to Neptune anytime soon—only that astronauts serve a need that is too often disparaged. Every time an automated marvel like Voyager is in the news, op-ed writers argue that this is the way to go, that robot expeditions are much cheaper and more rational than human ones.

Rationality is not the issue here. What rational need is there, for example, for Voyager to tell us the temperature on Triton? Our need is poetic: an urge to find, imagine, and describe the coldest of all known worlds.

The moon landings were called stunts, because robot landers could have done their scientific work much more cheaply. But we were not paying for facts. We were expressing a deep human need—the same one that drove our ancestors to wander out of Africa and people every corner of the globe. Two peoples whose history involves conquest of a vast natural frontier, the Americans and the Russians, are the ones that would do the same in space.

Someday we shall colonize the solar system, building a new civilization with energy and ores from the sun and the asteroids, far beyond the ecological constraints of one planet. But this is not what directly motivates us now. The short-term benefits are less tangible, more emotional.

They include, for example, the image of the earth as an exquisite, fragile sphere suspended in a black void— and the knowledge that this photograph was taken by a homesick astronaut orbiting the dead moon. It is no coincidence that publication of this photo around the world was followed by an awakening of ecological consciousness and celebration of the first Earth Day.

The space program is driven, too, by the same psychological and financial motives that in other contexts lead to warfare. The same kind of people volunteer to join. It uses the same technology, and benefits the same economic interests. But in these moral ambiguities lies part of its survival value.

Those instincts will always be with us. There will always be those who are driven to risk their lives and to unleash power, testing themselves against an adversary that may be another tribe, or another frontier. The technocracy will not easily relinquish its power. But it does not particularly care whether it builds bombers or spaceships, "Star Wars" technology or moon colonies, so long as it remains in business. Let's keep it busy, and sublimate those instincts for war, with an activity that is at least harmless and exciting, at most a key to our future.

I think I can imagine where Dr. Taylor was coming from. Uneasy in his work of designing nuclear explosives, he found a way of putting the infernal devices in the service of a poetic adventure, a nuclear Odyssey.

It's just as well his rocket never got off the ground.

Its blast-off would have left a trail of radioactive fall-out. But the moral calculation at the heart of the scheme still holds.

Today there are scientists in the United States and Russia who want our two countries to join in sending astronauts on an expedition to Mars. Others say the trip would be too expensive, a highly inefficient way to gather facts. But what a powerful symbol for peace it would be, what a visionary way to redirect the impulses that led us to brandish rockets at one another, what an adventure.

Dr. Taylor will never gaze from Orion's porthole at the frigid disk of Pluto, but others will fly there on the wings of some more benign propulsion, solar power perhaps, in ships that will unfurl broad gossamer sails to catch the inexhaustible force of photons, stately galleons of the sun bearing the new explorers toward an endless frontier.

The
Blue Crystal

For Christmas my sister gave me Planet Earth as a tree ornament: a three-inch translucent globe, painted in the blues and greens of the seas and continents, suspended by a nylon thread.

There's a hole in Antarctica. "The ozone hole," my brother remarked. Actually, it's the tiny opening through which the artist had painstakingly painted the world on the interior of the glass, wielding her brush inside the little sphere.

It reminded me of the Christmas of 1968, when astronauts first orbited the moon. They read the Bible, their voices heard here on television from the void of space, and took color photos of the grandest Christmas ornament in existence, our lovely, fragile home planet.

At the National Air and Space Museum in Washington, there is a movie theater with an enormous curved screen that shows films made aboard the space shuttle. One of these is called *The Blue Planet.* I found it intensely moving. Later I thought about why. Anything filmed from a spaceship has to be exciting, especially when projected on a giant screen, but these images were more than that, stirring viewers even to tears of wonder, awe, and a strange mix of gratitude and protectiveness.

The earth, seen from space, is indeed the loveliest

thing there is, but how do we earthlings know that? How is it that I instinctively recognize this image, and with such an immediate, powerful sense of enchantment, when presumably it has never before, until this instant of our evolution, starting in the 1960s, been possible for any human to behold it?

I can speculate how it would have been an evolutionary incentive for our distant ancestors to be stirred to wonder by vistas of land and sea, beckoning with the promise of home, sustenance, freedom, and the expansion of the species. But they never lived with anything remotely resembling the amazing, luminous sphere that today the pioneers of our species can photograph from orbit.

Or I could essay a personal explanation, derived from a childhood of enchantment with globes (and Christmas ornaments). Here is the Platonic ideal of the globe, shorn of its transitory excrescences of geographical names and borders.

In the lobby of the grade school I went to was a wonderful globe, perhaps four feet across, made of glass and illuminated by a lamp in the middle. I associate it, however, also with boring geography lessons and with the ferocious headmaster who scowlingly forbade anyone even to think about touching it.

Any kid bold enough to lay hands on the precious orb, let alone succumb to the temptation to send it spinning, would have been subjected to the headmaster's favorite punishment, which was, in those days before politically correct child rearing, a series of sharp taps on the knuckles with a ruler.

"Put out your hand," the old man would command, in his slithery voice with its British accent that was said behind his back to be fake (he was Canadian), grinning slyly and reaching beneath the jacket of his double-breasted suit for the ruler he carried everywhere.

No, there has to be some other explanation for why these images of our planet in space evoke such a shock of recognition. I don't have it, although one association that comes to mind is the concluding image from Stanley Kubrick's *2001*—that cosmic fetus, floating in space inside a transparent sphere, heading toward the earth.

Science fiction aside, some very important things began to change when the astronauts took those first photos of the home planet, especially the ones taken from the vicinity of the moon—far enough, though only a baby step in cosmic terms, to show how small and precious the place really is.

The image became a symbol, and a cause too, of the environmental movement that came alive in the following years. It also illustrated the absurdity of war, of the people on one side of this magical sphere bickering with the people on the other side. Indeed, the two peoples with the readiest access to this image, the two nations that sent explorers into space with cameras, no longer fear each other.

Spheres have always been images of perfection, even before we knew for sure that we lived on one. Our ancestors speculated that the heavens were composed of them, and today we still hang them on Christmas trees.

But one of them is infinitely special. Even when our descendants, some of them, are natives of space colonies and a "terraformed" Mars, and perhaps of planets around other stars, they will still experience that same instinctive thrill when, returning perhaps as tourists, they look from the windows of their spacecraft and see the earth for the first time—that same shock of recognition I experience when I see a film like *The Blue Planet.*

Meanwhile, I've hung my Christmas globe from a window frame, where it glows in the sunlight with the magic of the real thing.

1-800-LUCIFER

In the old days the Devil called door-to-door, a traveling salesman with a bag of temptations tucked under one scaly wing. But traveling salesmen are no longer cost-efficient. Instead, canvassers telephone at dinnertime. Stockbrokers. Charitable groups. Politicians. Why should the Devil waste his time on the road when he can stay in his cozy warm office and just pick up the phone?

If you're not on his list, don't despair. He has a soul-free number. Crave something that only he can provide? Don't wait. Just dial 1-800-LUCIFER. He'll be happy to fax you a contract.

When the Devil calls, I'll know what to say. One evening the phone will ring and his husky voice will be on the line, with a string of offers he thinks I can't refuse.

"Can I interest you in power?" he'll purr. "How about fame and glory? Infinite wealth? The secret of life? The love of numerous beautiful women? A Porsche? The Nobel Prize? The White House?"

No thanks, Mr. Devil. Not what I have in mind. Please take me off your list. But then he'll get to the point. "Would you be interested," he'll say, "in *immortality?*"

Why sure. Absolutely. Where do I sign?

Immortality hits the spot. If it's not available, I'll settle for 10,000 years, then apply for an extension. Three score and ten, the Biblical span, is for the birds. It was established in a preindustrial era: pre-Gutenberg, pre-newspaper, precomputer, pre- pretty much anything except sex and war and eating. Not much happened in those days, besides the occasional battle or orgy; not much was known, there wasn't much to read, and nobody went anywhere—so it was possible for one person to traverse the limits of available experience, read all the books, and master all the sciences in one standard lifetime.

The last person who did that was Thomas Jefferson, and even then he needed to be a genius and a workaholic. Today even a workaholic can spend 70 years mastering just one branch of one science—and then bang! Time's up.

Immortality is the only way I'll ever catch up on my reading. I'll even get around to Henry James. And there'll be time to travel to every country in the world, at my rate of two or three a year, after which, by the time I run out of countries, a couple of centuries from now, it will be possible to move on and buy tickets to other planets and stars.

I can't wait. Meanwhile I'll be reading the daily paper every day forever. For some people that could get boring after a century or two, but I'm an addict. I've been doing it for 30 years already and still the urge never lets up—the compulsion to find out *what happens next*. So put me down for an eternal subscription.

Faust was right on. We're talking serious temptation here. Must remember, though, to specify the option of eternal youth. The goddess Aurora forgot, in the Greek myth in which she asked Zeus to give her lover Tithonus eternal life, period. He got more and more withered and shrunken as he got more and more old, until after a few hundred years there was nothing much left of him at all.

Tithonus is still around somewhere, but all he is now is a grasshopper.

I'm ready to sign. The Devil hasn't called yet, though. And calling 1-800-LUCIFER turns out to be major frustration. A sepulchral voice says, "If you are calling in reference to power, press 1 now. If you are calling in reference to riches, press 2. . . ."

I press 6 for immortality. The voice says, "We are sorry. All our lines are busy at this time. Please hold, and the next available demon will be happy to take your call." Music comes on the line: the damnation scene from *Don Giovanni*. I wait and wait. They sure are busy down there. Must be all those folks selling their souls for posts in the Clinton administration.

But I must have fallen asleep at my desk. The phone is ringing. I answer it expectantly. "Good evening," says the chirpy voice. "I'm calling from the Audubon Society."

The Airplane
of
Youth

The next best thing to immortality is to keep traveling, as I do, and never look back. It seems to work. Travel writers, for instance, do not age. To travel is to be reborn. Those who constantly go on journeys, being lucky enough to write about them for a living, are always a step ahead of that old devil, time. Stop somewhere too long, or go home, and time catches up, pins you down, etches its lines on your face. Keep going, lose track of time—and time loses track of you.

Ponce de León and the other adventurers who voyaged in search of the fountain of youth had it only half right. It was the quest and not its goal that kept them young. It was when they gave up and came home that they withered.

Look at the jacket photo on any travel book; the author resembles Dorian Gray. Take Paul Theroux. He's been riding trains and kayaks around the world incessantly, for as long as I can remember, and he looks not a day older than when he started.

The theory of relativity lets science fiction writers imagine space explorers returning to an earth where centuries have passed while they themselves have aged only months. This could be a problem for the travel writer of the future, whoever sets out to do for interstellar spacecraft what Mr. Theroux did for trains and kayaks. Knowing that, by the time he returns, his publisher, agent, and readers will all be long dead, he'll just have to hope that a public still exists for his latest book on strange customs among the denizens of Sirius.

Earthbound travelers enjoy a less drastic form of relativity, psychological in nature. This is because travel replicates the experience of early childhood. Hence my theory of travel relativity.

For the infant everything is new, a source of delight or terror. Every day is an eternity of wonder. A child's existence is like a journey in which every word and sign is a puzzle to be learned and deciphered, every custom is a challenge to be mastered, every sound, color, and taste is strange and marvelous.

So it is for the traveler—and the farther one goes the better. Asia, say. There an American may become as wide-eyed, open-minded, and naive as a baby. In effect, he cannot speak or read. He strives constantly to understand. He does not know the right way to behave. He hardly even knows how to eat—cross-legged on the floor, with chopsticks, sampling mysterious and unprecedented flavors.

The late food writer James Beard once speculated that the popularity of Big Macs could be explained by their resemblance to baby food—their squishiness and sweetness appealing to an infantile streak in this young nation. Be that as it may, an American venturing into the cuisine of most older societies (England excepted) feels like an excited toddler weaned from a bland, bottled diet to brave the spicy grownup fare.

Speechless as an infant when I travel to the lands of exotic flavors, I open my ears to the Babel around me, straining to recognize phrases, and to mimic them. Given enough childlike persistence, and perhaps a little help from indulgent natives, one day I open my mouth, and sounds come out: something like *"Birru kudesai"* in Japan, or *"Mek-ju chuseyo"* in Korea. And what do you know, it works! The waiter understands, and brings beer. *"Domo arigato"* or *"Kamsa hamnida,"* I burble, mightily pleased with myself.

It's a thrill, learning to talk. And in most countries (France excepted) an American attempting a phrase in the local tongue is greeted with the kind of delighted approval that adults bestow on an infant's first words. They think it's really cute.

Travel doesn't just broaden the mind. First it empties it, clears it, opens it to everything new, to the world of a growing child, a world of curiosity and enchantment. The fountain of youth was an erroneous metaphor. It cannot be a fixed location. Better to speak of the river of youth—or the ocean, the railroad, the freeway. Behold the contemporary Ponce de León, embarking on the airplane of youth.

And then the voyager returns. He "catches up." Time catches up.

Recently, truth emulated science fiction when a Soviet cosmonaut returned after a year in space to a land that was no longer, among other things, Soviet.

Similarly, even a brief journey abroad can leave one exposed to the hazards of future shock. Instant senescence. After that delicious interval of peripatetic rejuvenation, one awakens to a rude present of burning cities and confounded politicians.

Paul Theroux has the right idea. Get back on that train, plane, or kayak. The world is still big and new enough for many more years of childhood.

THE BEAST *in the* TREES

The Sachems

The whine of a mosquito circling my ear on a hot night is a sound that awakens weird memories of summer camp. Have anthropologists studied that institution? They'd better. Like boarding schools and monasteries, camps evolve in curious tribal patterns. Camp Adirondack, where I spent four summers, was a singularly strange specimen, its culture a thick blend of pseudo-Indian lore, militarism, and nature worship.

The 15 cabins (which, to save money or harden endurance, lacked electricity and window screens—hence the omnipresent mosquito's hum) were named after Indian nations. Counselors, however, were addressed by their first names with the prefix "Sir," as if they were knights. The camp director, who the rest of the year was a National Guard colonel and commandant of a boys' marching society in New York City, was called Sir Bill.

Bugle calls punctuated the day, from reveille to taps. At 6 P.M. the cabin tribes assembled in martial formation and reported to Sir Bill or his deputy, Sir Don ("Mohawk all present and accounted for, sir!"), after which a cannon was fired and the flag lowered.

I was loyal to my cabin and my sporting faction, the Blues, who contended against the Whites. The camp was also divided between braves and squaws. Fridays after dark everyone gathered in a forest clearing below a cliff, around a bonfire. The squaws, boys new to the camp, had to sit on the ground in back and wear blankets over their heads.

When a brave saw a squaw, he was supposed to say "Ugh!" For a squaw to become a brave, he first had to perform certain tasks, such as observing a vow of silence and memorizing the "Ode to the Great Spirit." Then, during the next Friday ceremony, he was blindfolded and initiated inside the sachems' tepee.

The sachems were counselors who, for the occasion, wore loincloths and long black wigs, painted their bodies and faces, and spoke in high-pitched, mocking tones. They resembled devils. The initiant had to endure their taunts, recite the brave's catechism, and eat sachem food, a revolting paste whose ingredients were a closely guarded secret of the sachem cult. Were I to recreate it today, I would stir together equal parts black pepper, curry powder, salt, vinegar, Tabasco sauce, and mustard. "Hee-hee-hee!" cried the sadistic priesthood as I slurped and gagged on this concoction. "You like sachem food?"

When I passed this ordeal, I was entitled to attend the Friday ritual as a brave, sitting in front on a log, carrying my blanket folded on my shoulder, wearing a headdress with feathers, and yelling "Ugh!" at my slower campmates among the squaws. The feathers were awarded for achievement in other camp activities. If you lasted there four summers, as I did, you garnered a lot of feathers.

All this sounds awful (and politically incorrect). In some ways it was—particularly when the boys themselves introduced an element of *Lord of the Flies* savagery into their relations, which the younger counselors often overlooked, even colluded in. To my lasting shame, I was a ringleader in one such persecution, whose victim was a pudgy little whiner, Chester Gold (not his real name). The grandson of an illustrious robber baron, Chester aroused the resentment of the rest of us in Mohawk Cabin by flaunting his ownership of expensive gadgets like a movie camera and a Minox. I composed a song, to the tune of "Cheers, cheers for old Notre Dame," which started: "Tears, tears, for young Chester Gold, / You take the Chester, I'll take the Gold, / Send him out to run ten laps / And don't let him stop till he collapse." This became quite a hit, which the entire camp took to singing at lunch in the mess hall until Sir Bill banned it. But there was justice in this world. The following summer, as the youngest boy in Huron Cabin, I became the butt of a trio of bullies, and I still harbor fantasies of revenge against my chief tormenter, a burly 12-year-old sociopath by the name of Jim ("Jimbo") Mainzer (his real name; so go ahead and sue me, Jimbo—make my day).

But it wasn't always awful. The camp had a stupendous saving grace: its site, a peninsula on New York's Lake George, opposite a majestic vista of unpeopled mountains rising steep from the pure water.

It made good use of this setting—hiking and sailing, nature walks, plenty of swimming, and a Sunday ritual that contrasted with Friday's paganism as day to night. All the boys (attired in the camp's blue and white uniform) would walk soberly single file along a path by the lake to a huge flat rock furnished with log benches and a cross made of two logs lashed together.

There, a portable harmonium was set up and a form of Christian service was conducted in the open air, the congregation of campers and counselors facing the cross and the clear, vast lake, singing "Onward, Christian

Soldiers." We had the sun in our faces and the breeze in our hair. It was better than any church.

I wonder now how all this was invented, this culture with its complex traditions and three sacred sites: the parade ground, the sachem circle, and the Christian rock. Some of it clearly reflected the mindset of Sir Bill, the soldier who owned the camp. The pseudo-Indian rites (and the high-tech conjuring tricks sometimes performed as demonstrations of sachem magic) were organized behind the scenes by one Sir Bob, a heavyset man in his thirties who took them very seriously.

But it was not, I think, so much a deliberate concoction, this anthropological hodgepodge, as an instinctive reenactment of some fundamental ancient patterns, fleshed out with bits of remembered lore and hokum, and flourishing in temporary isolation from modern society and particularly from female influence. Women seldom intruded in this place, and if one did it was the custom to raise a general alarm, the words shouted in relay from one end of the peninsula to the other: "Fire in the icebox!"

I don't think our parents realized how odd the camp was, how bizarre its tribal practices. There must be men now in their thirties and forties who still remember it with loathing; others, with keen nostalgia; and others with both, as I do—recalling both the savage rituals and the natural splendor.

Several years ago I learned the following: a boy who had attended this camp grew up and became wealthy. He found out that, after the death of Sir Bill, the camp had closed, the property (thousands of acres) left unused. So keenly did he remember his summers there that he bought the place and started up the camp again, with himself as director.

That's all. I don't know if he reinstated the pagan, Christian, and martial ceremonies. I don't know if the lake is still as beautiful as I remember it. I should go back and see.

Meanwhile, when I read of the so-called men's movement, that much-ridiculed quest for masculine roots by way of forest treks, drums, campfires, and tribal bonding rituals, I feel I have already been there, a pre-adolescent Robert Bly under the aegis of the sachems of Camp Adirondack. The frustrated men who drum and bellow in the woods today are only trying to return to Sir Bill's summer camp.

Chief Salamander

In mythology, salamanders are flickering creatures that live in fire. In Karel Capek's apocalyptic novel *War with the Newts,* they are large, intelligent sea-dwellers who mimic human technology and culture, build cities and factories on the ocean floor as they multiply by the billion, and eventually, in a radio broadcast to the human race from their leader, Chief Salamander, announce their plans to dismantle and submerge the continents, in order to expand their living space.

When I was nine, on the other hand, I had a pet newt, which never did much of anything until one day it bestirred itself to crawl into a crack in the floor, from which, to my dismay, it never emerged.

Years later I built a house. As we dug the cesspool, the rig uncovered a burrow, several feet underground, where four spotted salamanders were hibernating. One was dead. The others—exquisite, plump, torpid black and yellow creatures—survived thanks to Bruce, a carpenter who happened to be standing by. He saw the creatures and stopped the work long enough to evacuate them in a leaf-filled spackle bucket.

Bruce also happened to love snakes. At home he had a collection of them in terrariums. He proposed to set up a terrarium there for the three salamanders. I checked with a couple of experts, my friends Larry and Andy, who agreed that the displaced amphibians should overwinter at Bruce's, it being too late in the season for them to find a new frost-free burrow.

I felt responsible for the little guys. My house had uprooted theirs. I had tried to site the house, on a hill far from any wetlands, where it would do the least damage to anything natural except for a lot of scrub oak. But salamanders, I learned, can crawl hundreds of yards from the ponds where they spawn, to seek out winter quarters.

From time to time that winter, I made the rounds between Andy's compost heap, to dig up some of the earthworms that he feeds his own snakes, and Bruce's house, to present the worms to the sleepy trio. In the spring I brought the salamanders back to the woods behind my house and set them free. Characteristically, they just sat there. But when I returned an hour later they were gone. Presumably they found their way to whatever seasonal pond they frequent and, with their descendants, are still in the neighborhood.

My impression, then, was of a somewhat sluggish, even comatose animal. But one March night, on a salamander-spotting walk sponsored by the Nature Conservancy, I learned otherwise. For a couple of weeks each year, when the weather changes as it just had, these otherwise somnolent creatures spring into a frenzy of social activity.

Andy led us to one of the shallow ponds (dry much of the year, and therefore free of predatory fish) where they migrate to perform their mating rituals. The pond was seething with salamanders—hundreds of them, as well as peepers and other frogs—darting, writhing, dancing in the beams of our flashlights.

It was, in microcosm, an awesome sight. There was a whole world in that little pond, a teeming social order, a mysterious knowledge that led these creatures every spring from their hiding places in the surrounding woods to converge on that particular spot and burst into their dance of propagation.

It is, too, a terribly fragile world. I had inadvertently, on my hilltop, displaced a household, a salamanders' winter rental. A developer, unknowingly or uncaringly bulldozing the site of one of these seasonal ponds, can wipe out a whole society. The pond we visited is safe; Andy, a bullion dealer in New York when he is not pursuing his herpetological interests on Long Island and in other, wilder places, had bought the site and placed it in a conservation trust. But other breeding spots, unluckily existing on valuable real estate, are being lost forever.

Watching the flickering of these nocturnal beings, I understood how their motion could have been confused in ancient times with fire. I also thought of Capek's book and its strange vision of a powerful nation of giant salamanders colonizing and enlarging the oceans.

Published in 1937, *War with the Newts* is understood as a political satire against fascism. Today, I think, it can also be given an ecological reading. I went back to the book and looked up Chief Salamander's broadcast to humanity, which he croaks into his underwater microphone:

"Hello, you people! Don't get excited. We have no hostile intentions toward you. We only need more water, more coasts, more shallow water to live in. There are too many of us. There is not space enough for us on your coasts any longer.

Therefore we must break down your continents. From them we shall make bays and islands all round.

"In this way the length of coast in the world can be increased five times. We shall make new shallow places. We can't live in the deep sea. We shall need your land to fill up the deep parts.

"We have nothing against you, but there are too many of us. For the time being you can move inland. You can withdraw to the mountains. The mountains will be pulled down last."

There is poetic justice in this vision of salamanders pushing back human civilization to create more wetlands. In reality, of course, it is we that there are too many of. We may have no hostile intentions toward salamanders and the rest of nature, but there is not space enough any longer for all of us.

Thanks to people like Andy and groups like the Conservancy, some space, at least, has been set aside for the beings that lived there before we multiplied across the landscape.

The eagerest participants in that March walk were children, whose generation will inherit this responsibility—perhaps, if the keen interest of these kids is any gauge, with greater care than ours has shown.

Cloud
of
Husbands

A cloud of husbands was droning by the eaves. I don't bother them and they don't bother me, though they far outnumber the rest of my household, which comprises 2 humans, 2 cats, 6 moths, 12 spiders (the cats of the insect world), 24 flies, 1 computer, 2 squirrels under the roof deck, and 1 audacious mouse who raids the cat food and gets away with it.

One spring day came the musical cloud. The warm breeze through the windows carried a sound that was like a distant chorus of table saws, or an orchestra tuning up. I put down my newspaper and stepped onto the porch. Thousands of bees were swirling in a whirlwind by the side of the house.

Some of them would alight on the shingles and soffits, checking out the possibilities and somehow signaling their findings to the hierarchy within the swarm. Slowly the cloud condensed toward a spot where there is a narrow gap between shingle and trim, until they formed a pulsating clump, clinging to the house and each other, working their way through the crack to the hollow interior of the eaves, which has been their home ever since.

I could drill through the wall to the hive and take some of their honey. But that would be trespassing. It's their community, an industrious one with a busy airport, where flurries of workers come and go all day long in the pursuit of nature's commerce. They don't venture to the interior of my house, which has nothing to do with their jobs, and I don't intrude in theirs.

One day a year later, the cloud reconstituted itself. There was the same overwhelming sound, the same tornado of insects. After a while, it divided. Half coalesced back in the eaves, half in the crook of a nearby tree, throbbing there in a football-size clump, a new colony with its own newly anointed queen packed at the center of her thousands of attentive husbands. When I looked again an hour later, the second swarm had gone—following word from its scouts of a suitable crevice in, perhaps, someone else's roof.

There was a tremendous sense of power in the sight and sound of this purposeful swarm. It is part of a will stronger than anything of ours. When we worry about the death of nature, we lose sight of this implacable will in nature's heart, which expresses itself constantly in a thousand ways around us, rebounding where we pause in our activities and infiltrating each chink of our settlements.

The worst we can do, with our buildings and bombs and pollution, is momentarily diminish it, partially interrupt its design. As we drive ourselves toward extinction, causing any number of other species to precede us into oblivion, nature waits, indifferent to the tragedy. In the long run, nature's run, there will always be something left after we're gone, even if it is only rodents or insects, which in a few million years will re-evolve, as they did after the extinction of the dinosaurs, to reconstitute as full a panoply of natural diversity as was here before we began building our cities and machines.

One thing about our successors, if we do ourselves

in—the thinking descendants of mice or bees or whatever: they may be no more gentle than we are, but they will be less destructive, without industrial technology, because we have already extracted virtually all the metals and fossil fuels that lie accessibly near the earth's surface. That is an endowment we have used up, an experiment that nature won't repeat. Those who follow us, for better or for worse, will have to make do without iron and oil, and content themselves with farming, woodcarving, storytelling, and other ecologically benign pursuits.

Meanwhile, the bees here go about their business—happily, maybe, if the word has any meaning in their experience of the world, but at least purposefully, and wholly unaware and uncaring that the structure they inhabit functions also as my own house. Perhaps we, too, unwittingly inhabit some level of complexity beyond beehive and house, beyond cell and body and mind, as sure and yet ignorant of where we are as my opportunistic neighbors in the eaves.

Nymphs
in
Light

When painters rave about the light of eastern Long Island, where I live, they often compare it to Italy's, and talk about the influence of the water. The adjacent ocean and bays are said to mediate the sunlight and throw it back into the atmosphere, giving the sky, more than in other places, a special radiance that seems to come from all directions, saturating the moisture-laden air, and magically intensifying the blues and greens in the landscape.

Something like that. I've heard several painters talk this way, and—while I'm not sure it makes sense in scientific, optical terms—I know what they mean. The only place I remember seeing light like ours is Italy, and there may well be a particular atmospheric and aquarian effect that happens only on certain peninsulas and islands.

The light comes and goes. To understand how it works, one would have to be an artist, physicist, and meteorologist rolled into one. It seems to happen most strikingly at cloudless, windless times in the long evenings of the late spring and summer.

It's no accident, of course, that the first outsiders to come here (after the Indians, Bonackers, and whalers) were artists. They came for the light, and also for the variety of landscape, remarkable in such a small geographical area, that, in another context, brings organizations like the Nature Conservancy, whose mission is ecological diversity, to focus on this spot.

The artists kept coming for a hundred years—at least until the area's fame and popularity, which they had started, began driving property values out of the reach of many. Even overdevelopment hasn't yet spoiled the light. It's only made life more hectic, to the point that we often don't notice it any more.

If I had been lucky enough to be born an artist, I would have taken my easel yesterday evening to a secret spot near my house, a glacial kettlehole that is almost perfectly hemispheric in form, like an amphitheater, with a family of beech trees, large and small, growing on its east slope. The deer hang out there at night. It's crisscrossed by the paths they make in the forest floor. A deer skull lies alone (no other bones are near; the foxes must have carried them off) in the exact center of the kettlehole floor, as if placed there for some ritual of sylvan devotion. During the day, the hollow is a timeless spot where nothing moves.

Not being an artist, I can only draw the picture in my mind and, from the other half of my brain, spill a few words. One word that has the wrong modern connotations but will suffice, in its original sense, is nymph. I can see how the Greeks, before science interfered with the natural generation of myth, figured that certain trees had to be inhabited by humanlike spirits.

The light did that, settling from the west through the budding oak and dogwood branches and appearing to single out the silver trunks of the beeches, with their oddly shifting angles (slanting one way as they grew, then another) that remind me of the undulations in a painting (Italian) of pagan spirits dancing serenely in a sun-dappled meadow.

The Grass
Is
Screaming

Whenever I mow the grass around my house (a patch of order that mediates between architecture and nature), I remember a story I once read in a science fiction magazine. It was about an inventor who made a device that could detect, and transpose down to audible range, sounds of extremely high frequency never before heard by human ears. Trying it out for the first time, he put on the headphones and heard screams.

The sound, which resembled the cries of thousands of children being slaughtered, grew louder until it was almost unbearable, then faded, grew loud again, faded again. The horrified inventor looked up and saw, through his window, a boy on a lawnmower. The mower passed near his window, receded, approached again, receded again. . . .

Not everyone believes I feel guilty using a lawnmower, not even when I repeat the story of the screaming blades of grass. I'm told I am rationalizing my procrastination. But it's true, especially when I decimate the clover, which tries so hard, growing back in great pudgy clumps between mowings.

Later, though, there is also pride—in a job accomplished, in the imposition of a certain degree of order. It may be like the pride of a butcher in a neatly dressed carcass, of a developer in a razed grove—or the pride of an artist.

Creation goes hand in hand with destruction. Like morality, art has to do with knowing where to stop. The sculptor destroys part of the stone to reveal the statue. The painter violates the purity of the white canvas, disorders the pure hierarchy of colors in their separate tubes. The gardener weeds, the writer edits.

The other day I created a footpath in the woods. I created nothing, only destroyed. I made a vacuum. I took my chainsaw and killed young trees that otherwise might have grown and flourished for many years, outliving me. Then I pulled out all the smaller plants in my way. I took hundreds of lives.

But I love my new footpath, my little bypass. It is a space that brings out the nymphlike beauty of the trees alongside it, and is beautiful too in its identity: a potential for action, a passage from home to desired destination, a way. It is intended for a life more complex and particular than those that were sacrificed for it, which are repeated by the million in the surrounding woods.

That, anyway, is how I presume to decree matters as a member of the species that alone makes choices over the lives of others. My cat, who follows me down the path, knows that he sees a bird, and what it means to him, but cannot question what it means to others, and to itself. If he could kill it he would, every time. It would give him untroubled pleasure to do so. He is not called upon to choose.

In planning my footpath, I replayed a dilemma of two years before, when I cleared what is now my driveway. After each day's cutting, I sat in judgment over the next stretch, marking with red ribbon those trees it would be necessary to fell. In the morning, I would review their sentences and consider whether any could be reprieved. I told the doomed oaks and hickories that their death would be compensated for in greater life for their spared fellows, with more light and nutrients left to share.

Now they are logs for my wood stove. The driveway winds, avoiding the largest and healthiest trees. I am glad it is only trees I make these choices for. I would not like to be a general in a battle, or a doctor in an epidemic, practicing triage.

Many more trees—fir, pine, and cedar—were felled to make the lumber with which I built my house. I presumed to exchange their order in nature for one that proceeded from my mind, my design. That kind of decision goes with the human territory. When I thought the lumber was used efficiently, I was untroubled. When it was wasted—when a rafter was cut the wrong length, say, and had to be scrapped—I suffered guilt. A lesser but still useful purpose inherited the scrap; it goes, sooner or later, into the wood stove, and somewhere there is a little more oil or gas for someone else to burn.

The summer after I finished my house, I happened to be driving in the West, where the fir and cedar came from. Whole mountains in British Columbia and Washington were clear-cut—a pathetic, obscene vista. It was not the use of the wood that was troubling, but the lack of proportion. The lumber companies did not know when to stop.

It's sometimes hard to know. Proportion is a subjective quality that depends on who and where the beholder happens to be. For some people, cutting even one tree is too many. For others, clearing a whole mountainside is a responsible act so long as it is reseeded. For a New Yorker, spending $12 in a restaurant is an act of thrift. For a Russian, the same $12 is a shocking extravagance. Having read that the per capita income in rural China is $150 a year, I developed the mental tic of framing expenses in terms of Chinese incomes. A restaurant meal: one Chinese month. Car repair: two Chinese years. Of course, I don't live in China. For the time being at least, proportions are different; troubling though the disparity may be, there's not that much I can do about it.

But the other day I read that someone in an auction at Sotheby's paid $88,000 for a rare teddy bear. Five hundred and eighty-seven Chinese years for a teddy bear. One might imagine some superrich country, some super-Kuwait, where restaurant meals cost $100,000, a car repair costs $1 million, and the "high-priced teddy," as the newspaper headline called it, would be at home. In the world we live in, the set of proportions we share, it is a symptom of something badly out of whack, in the same category as Hamptons real estate, the $17 million Jasper Johns, the Stealth bomber.

Having finished the task of writing an essay, I'll proceed to another I've been postponing all week: mowing the grass. Though it requires this periodic act of violence, though it cost me several Chinese years plus a number of days of my own labor, I take pleasure in this compromise I demand of nature. But I'll detour around the wildflowers, and look out for the turtle I rescued from the mower's path last time.

As for that teddy bear, I hope the buyer's dog eats it.

The Torrents
of
Sex

The call of the peeper or tree frog that we hear on spring nights in the country is sung by the male of the species in an exhausting tour de force of courtship that takes place in the vicinity of ponds. The louder and longer this bite-size Tristan holds forth, the more alluring he becomes to the silent female.

I was thinking of him one night while I was singing in the shower. It was a fine old reggae tune by Lee Perry that I was caterwauling, "Roast Fish and Cornbread." Its refrain goes like this: "Roast fish and cornbread, yeah? Roast fish and cornbread, yeah!"

And suddenly I stopped and said, "Aha! Now I know why men sing in the shower."

Science Times had that day reported a treacherous experiment in which a recording of a male peeper's song was played through a loudspeaker while some real males held forth nearby. When the scientists turned the volume up, the listening females fell all over themselves trying to get into the box that contained the loudspeaker, abandoning their hapless suitors in their zeal to meet this amphibian Elvis. (Something like that must have happened the first time a pop singer hit on the idea of amplifying his voice and guitar.)

The song of the male frog, which requires prodigious

energy to belt out, establishes that he is strong and healthy. Females instinctively desire the singer with the greatest volume and stamina, so that her tadpoles will inherit his vigor—and incidentally, in the case of the sons, his musical instinct.

Which brings me to the question, why do men sing in the shower? Some theorists attribute this behavior to the acoustics of the shower stall, which are held to amplify the voice in a manner so gratifying to its owner, as well as in a privacy so remote from any critical ears, that even the shiest and least musical can't resist the impulse there to burst into song.

But does that theory hold water, so to speak? For one thing, men do not sing while they defecate. Never. Not even in restroom stalls, where, despite their acoustical resemblance to shower stalls, even the most audaciously lyrical confine their verses to written form.

Nor do we normally sing in the bath. Nor do women habitually sing in the shower, at least not loudly and often. The only exception I can think of is the female character in *South Pacific* who sings, "I'm gonna wash that man right out of my hair!" Significantly, as we shall see, she is singing her rejection of a man.

The acoustic theory, finally, begs the question, If men sing in the shower because we like to hear ourselves sing, *why* do we like to hear ourselves sing?

We must look for an explanation for an instinct that originated with our distant amphibian ancestors and evolved during the prehistoric flowering of our own species, so that it remains innate in men today, in the preverbal recesses of our minds, until triggered by the sound of rushing water.

I say preverbal, because it does not matter what the

words are. There is no objectively classifiable reason why I, for example, should sing, "Roast fish and cornbread, yeah?"—not even hunger, since I know I will have lasagna for dinner. Nor do I proceed logically to sing more lyrics of this particular song ("Breadnut and peanut, yeah? / Peanut and breadnut, yeah!") which is, in any case, the most verbally coherent of my shower repertoire.

No, the instinct is more ancient than words. Here is an early-hominid scenario to explain it:

The tribe has spent the winter huddled in furs in a cave. Once in a while the food runs out and the hunters have to go catch a mastodon, but otherwise no one has any energy or desire. All have grown exceedingly unkempt and smelly, caked with six months of grime and mastodon grease. The lack of deodorants, and the general winter depression, have discouraged romantic attachments.

Now it is spring. On the first hot day, tribespeople emerge from their caves, blinking in the sun, and run down to the nearest mountain torrent, where they throw aside their fetid furs and splash into the cool stream.

The men, in macho style, strut among the rapids and duck beneath the waterfall. The women dive about in the calmer pools. At some point, when everyone is good and clean, they begin to notice one another. The men grow aroused, and to attract the women's attention they burst into song. They stand in the waterfall and bellow while the women listen and make up their minds.

The men with the most sonorous voices are the most successful in this courtship and thus in passing on their genes, including the musical gene that causes them to vocalize when the noise of rushing water and the sensation of cleanliness triggers the instinct. Even to this day, that gene survives. Now that civilization has widened the scope of our mating rituals and brought us the comforts of central heating and daily showers, its function may be superfluous. But the instinct remains, drawing men into its primeval thrall whenever they turn on the shower.

The *Science Times* may not be ready for this theory, but never mind. The Italians have a saying, *"Se non e vero, e ben trovato."* Which I would translate roughly thus: "If it isn't true it should be."

Isn't there a song that goes, "It might as well be true . . ."?

I wasn't sure, so I asked my wife.

"I don't know," she said. "Sounds like something you sing in the shower."

THE
COUNTERFEITER

Art
versus
Art

In Switzerland, police recovered a stolen van Gogh, *Wheat Field with Sheaves,* and arrested the thieves when they attempted to exchange the painting for a $1.3 million ransom.

In SoHo, an art gallery showed pieces of the Berlin Wall.

Question: What is art?

a. Whatever a dealer says, a critic agrees, and a buyer believes.

b. A more durable alternative to the Lindbergh baby.

c. A form of high-denomination currency.

d. Portable real estate.

e. A billionaire's boast.

f. A dilettante's alibi.

g. An endangered species.

I used to live in a part of New York City that has been transformed by art, fashion, and greed. Twenty years ago, it was a neighborhood of mostly Italian and Portuguese heritage. There were also some artists, real ones, in low-rent tenements or in illegal lofts in the nearby Cast-Iron District.

The news that artists had "discovered" the area

made it fashionable, and it was renamed SoHo. Galleries and restaurants proliferated. Two guys named Dean and DeLuca opened a little store called The Cheese Shop. Lots of people who weren't artists decided they wanted to live in lofts. Some were rezoned so that only artists could legally occupy them.

It's still an attractive neighborhood, but rising rents have bled away much of its character and commercial life. On weekends the streets are thronged with tourists. Dean and DeLuca has bloomed into a palace of excess. Most of the Italian and Portuguese stores have been replaced by boutiques and antique shops. The amount of rent a business is willing to pay for commercial space seems to rise in inverse proportion to the usefulness of the objects it sells.

On my street there used to be a pharmacy, a furniture repair shop, a Knights of Columbus hall, a Portuguese travel agency, and a television repair shop. The first three are now restaurants. The other two appear to be art galleries.

There's something fishy about those galleries. Every couple of weeks, one or the other has an opening party, which looks like fun. But the rest of the time, nobody but the owners ever goes there. Nobody ever buys the "art." I use quotation marks because the paintings are not just bad, they are zilch: characterless rectangles of canvas or linoleum, all one color, or crisscrossed like tic-tac-toe grids. Their presence on gallery walls and price lists certifies them as art—but for what purpose?

They exist, I think, to establish an alibi: so that someone can say, "I am an artist," or "I run an art gallery," or "I qualify for an artist-in-residence-zoned loft."

Art can be its own worst enemy. It can make a place so trendy that real artists can no longer afford the rents.

Except for the few whose work is certified as a good investment, who are like engravers in an avant-garde mint. Each brush stroke is worth a thousand dollars. The piece becomes a news item. Is it a good painting? Hard to tell any more. The image is overshadowed by the story of who paid how much money for it at Sotheby's. A museum or collector buys it for a sum that might have been used to subsidize the work of many other artists of equal or greater talent. The collector (i.e., investor) locks it away where no one can see it; in the museum its notoriety attracts thieves and disgruntled lunatics with knives.

Question: What happens when you see a painting by (for example) Jasper Johns?

a. You're intensely moved by the profound beauty, passion, and wisdom of this immortal work.

b. You know that it sold at auction for $17 million, and you're filled with respect and admiration for the guy who paid the $17 million. He is a real winner.

c. You have to hand it to the guy who used to own it, who sold it for 1,000 times what he paid for it. Some people have all the luck.

d. You honestly wonder why it cost so much. You don't get it.

e. You think the art market has gone mad. Never have so few paid so much for so little.

f. Ha-ha, you think, every time Jasper Johns does a new painting, he must be laughing all the way to the bank.

g. You make invidious comparisons. For the price of this one painting, you could send 1,000 students to art school. You could build a museum. You could house 3,000 homeless families for a year. You could save a rain forest. Or (let's be fair) you could pay off one two-thousandth of one percent of the national debt. You could pitch in to help build a Stealth bomber, maybe pay for the landing gear plus the coffeemaker.

h. You think about stealing this painting and holding it for ransom.

Like that van Gogh. What started as the inspiration of a neglected visionary ends up as a $50 million investment vehicle, or as an empty frame in a museum preyed upon by razor-wielding thieves.

Authenticity has become a rare and hoarded commodity, like gold. A television image is free (or via cable, if the monthly bill is divided by the number of images seen, it costs a thousandth of a cent). A reproduction of a painting in a book or magazine costs a few pennies. It may be possible to create a full-size reproduction, indistinguishable from the original object, for a few dollars. But the painting itself may sell for millions, so long as it is agreed to be the authentic original. If it is proved to be a forgery, its price drops to that of a curiosity. So does its status as an object of scholarship. But the image hasn't changed. Nothing has changed except our concept of what's real.

Quality counts for little next to authenticity, rarity, and fashion. A van Gogh sells for ten times the price of a Rembrandt. An inferior van Gogh sells for a million times the cost of an exact copy of a good one. Authenticity becomes the enemy of art. It is purchased as a form of security, like a stock certificate, to be hidden in a bank vault; or as a symbol of pride, to advertise the collector's or museum's status. Awe at the financial transaction eclipses awareness of the work. Its moral and physical integrity are both at risk. Looters hack statuary from its context. Thieves cut paintings from their frames, for ransom or for the hoard of some criminal connoisseur. Museums cancel traveling exhibitions because they cost too much to insure. Money is diverted from the traditional patronage of younger artists.

A modest proposal: let's abolish authenticity. Let's produce, in unlimited numbers, reproductions of art works that cannot be distinguished from the original—and destroy every record of which piece is in fact the original.

Museums will resist this idea, but we can talk them into it. Look, we'll say, now you can stop paying those humongous insurance premiums. Now you can expand your collections without limit. Think how much money you can make selling the reproductions. The whole museum can be one big gift shop. Everybody can buy a van Gogh.

And because nobody will know for sure which among the objects for sale is in fact the secret original, all will be free to imagine that they are the one who bought it. Everyone will be a happy collector. Licensed forgery, perfect and infinite, will democratize the art world and redeem the purity of the image.

Ah, Valpolicella!

Without meaning to, I once played a mean trick on a friend, a doctoral student of literature who prided himself on being a connoisseur of all things Italian, especially Italian wines.

In those days, to save money, I would buy wine by the gallon jug, decant it into five old bottles, and recork them until needed. It kept better that way.

As we sat down to a dinner of veal parmigiana, I poured my friend a glass from one of those recycled bottles, whose label he espied with delight. Before I thought to say anything, he took a sip, rolled the wine around his tongue, held the glass up to the light, and exclaimed fondly, "Ah, Valpolicella!"

Had I been more considerate, I would have let him believe the wine was as the label indicated. But I was too honest and naive to let the misunderstanding pass. I explained my rationale for having filled the Valpolicella bottle with Almaden Mountain Red.

My friend was not grateful for this information. The rest of the meal was marked by uncomfortable silences, as he turned over in his mind the suspicion that I had tricked him on purpose.

Though I really hadn't, I do take an interest in stories of hoaxsters and forgers who, out of greed, ambition, or mischief, put one over on the experts: the French students who concocted a "lost" Rimbaud poem that had Rimbaud scholars writing learned commentaries on this important discovery; Clifford Irving, whose autobiography of Howard Hughes fooled almost everyone but Mr. Hughes himself; the writer who tricked the editors of the *New York Times Magazine* into printing an article about his adventures among the Khmer Rouge, which he had invented out of whole cloth; the *Washington Post* reporter whose fabricated article fooled everyone so thoroughly that she won a Pulitzer Prize; the forger whose fake Grünewald was vouched for by eminent scholars and purchased for millions by the Cleveland Museum of Art; the author of the "Hitler diaries."

There is a wicked thrill to these stories. If a fraud can so bamboozle the experts, can it be that their expertise, too, is a bit of a fraud? Naturally the experts are angry when the text or work of art they have championed turns out to be fake. They blame the forger for muddying the scholarly waters and betraying professional ethics. They seldom question their own authority or assumptions. Unlike the forger, they usually remain in business.

Take the eminent historian who declared he would stake his reputation on the genuineness of the Hitler diaries. Though he lost that bet, the *New York Review of Books* still publishes him.

Hoaxes need not ruin reputations, but they should restore humility. They throw certain assumptions into question. It is assumed, for instance, that there is an inherent relationship between authenticity and quality which can be formally demonstrated, circumstances aside. If it's real it must be good, and vice versa.

When the supposed Grünewald was thought to be truly the work of the sixteenth-century artist, scholars and museum goers experienced it as a masterpiece. When it turned out to be a modern forgery, it became merely a curiosity. The painted image hadn't changed. Chemical rather than stylistic analysis proved it a fake. Afterward, though, scholars began to notice stylistic discrepancies that had eluded them when they thought the work was genuine.

In art as in food, taste is not an exact science. There is (or used to be) a French television show on which a panel of distinguished food critics sample and comment on dishes cooked by guest chefs, one of whom, some years ago, was the daughter of Valéry Giscard d'Estaing, then president of France. Apparently a mischievous type, Mlle Giscard surreptitiously ruined her fish sauce by adding a large quantity of sugar. She wanted to show up the critics as frauds. Sure enough, each tasted the sabotaged dish and pronounced it delicious.

Later she told the press what she had done, throwing the unfortunate critics into ridicule and disgrace. They tried to point out, in defense, that it was hard to taste things while under the pressure of appearing on live TV, and that their palates had been further impaired by their awe at the chef's parentage.

For them, I see a kind of poetic justice in another story, according to which President Giscard himself ate something strange, without noticing, while on a state visit to Bangui, capital of the Central African Empire. Among the foibles of that country's ruler, the deranged Emperor Bokassa, was a taste for cannibalism, for which he kept a freezer specially stocked with parts of former political prisoners. When President Giscard came to dinner, so the story goes, the dish that he took to be veal was not veal.

Sometimes, as with my friend the connoisseur of Italian wines, it's true that what you don't know won't hurt you—not until you do know.

The Impostor

Like his colleague the counterfeiter, the impostor may fool us for money, for fun, or from an inner need, like an artist. Seeing no easy, legitimate way out of a frustrating life, he makes a brilliant leap into fantasy. He thrills to danger, living by his wits, on the edge, constantly finessing the catastrophe of exposure.

His victims are unconscious accomplices. The impostor is fulfilling their fantasy too. When he is exposed, they're shocked—but later they miss the con artist who enriched their lives. And others who hear of the truth find themselves admiring the bold impersonator, the fascinating chameleon. To be the audacious fellow who acts out a wild fantasy: that is itself a fantasy.

Audiences loved *Six Degrees of Separation*. So did those who saw the film *Chameleon Street*. Both are based on true stories about black youths who impersonated their way out of the ghetto, manipulating society's expectations, beguiling those more fortunate but less interesting.

Summer resorts like the Hamptons teem with the wealth and pretension that is fertile ground for impostors. So does Los Angeles. Occasionally a pretender is exposed to the fascination of the newspaper-reading public. Who is more interesting, the real Italian countess or the one who was in fact a secretary from New Jersey, who charmed her way from mansion to mansion with a phony accent and plenty of chutzpah? The fake is a better story—and, I would bet, a better dinner companion.

When Clifford Irving moved to East Hampton, freshly notorious for faking Howard Hughes's memoirs, he was greeted not as a rogue but as an engaging character, more fascinating than he could ever have been as author merely of his own books.

I had an interesting conversation with an impostor one morning when a man who claimed to be a movie producer phoned me out of the blue. I'd recently published a small book that, while it sold moderately well, wasn't providing much in the way of financial security. His call sounded like the answer.

"Hi Val," he drawled, in the familiar tone of an old friend. "This is Paul Irish in LA. President of ICP. You've heard of us?"

I hadn't, of course.

"Irish Coffee Productions," he explained. Now that name, plus the fact that he was calling at 8:30 A.M., which would have been 5:30 Los Angeles time, should have alerted me. But he was very charming, what he said was very appealing, and he had no rational motive for calling unless he was what he said he was.

He talked for half an hour, in a confident, mellow voice, about how he just loved my book, wanted to make it into a movie, wanted me to collaborate on the screenplay. "I believe in keeping the author creatively involved every step of the way," he said. "That's always been my guiding concept." Money, he intimated, was not his major concern, though he went into some detail about the budget he had in mind for the film, its schedule, and my fee.

It all sounded great. I gave him my agent's phone number, and she proved to be every bit as charmed and convinced as I was by the assured manner and interesting ideas of Paul Irish. True, she'd never heard of him or his oddly named company, but then Hollywood wasn't her field. Her next call would be to a Los Angeles agency that specialized in film rights.

It turned out that the names Paul Irish and ICP were equally unknown to the Hollywood agents. They promised to track down this mystery, and the next day they reported back with some surprising information.

Paul Irish, they said, was a chauffeur. He drove a limousine, and often his passengers were producers. While they talked business in the back, he would sometimes listen and think over what they'd said—and once in a while, he'd been known to make these phone calls . . .

Apparently the real producers had been talking about my book in the limo that night (I never did hear from them, though).

So my image of a powerful executive in a Hollywood suite faded to one of a chauffeur parked outside wherever producers get dropped off at 5 A.M., using the car phone to practice an imaginary role. He was, I guess, a kind of frustrated artist. Sure, Irish Coffee Productions sounds a bit rich in retrospect; so do the son of Sidney Poitier and the memoirs of Howard Hughes.

The Noble
Pretender

Occasionally a man may pretend to be what he is not, and artfully fool everyone he meets, not out of greed, mischief, or artistic zeal, but out of courage and a triumphant will to live. Such an ingenious survivor is Kassie Neou, who lived through the Khmer Rouge genocide in Cambodia. He survived by pretending—and by means of the storyteller's art. I met him when he spoke at an Amnesty International conference in New York. What he said there went something like this:

Until April 17, 1975, Kassie Neou, a slightly built, shy-looking man now in his forties, lived with his family in Phnom Penh and worked for the BBC. Part of his job was to translate Cambodian folktales for publication in English-language primers. This life ended the day the Khmer Rouge took over the capital and drove its population at gunpoint to labor in the countryside.

The new life of the revolutionary communes was one of constant exhaustion, hunger, and fear. Anyone who protested or faltered was taken away; so was anyone who appeared to be of a middle-class, educated background. It was announced that these people were at a "reeducation camp." Kassie Neou pretended he had been from the working class: a taxi driver.

One day he helped a fellow worker in the field, and

the man thanked him in French. It was a dangerous gesture of trust, which he matched with a reply in English. But they were not alone. He heard the voice of a teenage guard behind him: "You speak the language of the imperialists!" A pair of soldiers bound his arms and tied the rope to the handlebars of their bicycles, then pedaled 15 miles as he ran and stumbled between.

They arrived at a house where he was beaten and nearly suffocated with a plastic bag over his head, again and again, while his interrogators demanded he confess he was never a taxi driver. He stuck to his story. At night he and the other prisoners there were tied to stakes in the ground. Each night the guards would call out the names of several and take them to a nearby field, where their bodies would be seen the next day. This was the reeducation camp.

One night the guards called his name. He prepared himself to die, but instead they took him back to the guardhouse, where they ordered him to tell them a story. This was, he realized, a trick to make him reveal his middle-class background. All Cambodians love stories, but those of different classes would know different ones and tell them in different ways. It was his singular good luck that his work before the revolution had given him a wide knowledge of genuine peasant stories.

He told one, a traditional folktale. The guards fell silent and listened, wide-eyed. They had never heard anything so wonderful. The next night they brought him back for another story, and the following morning the day-shift guards called him in to tell it to them, too. Every night and day for three months, Kassie Neou, like Scheherazade, saved his life with a new story. It seems that even the teenage killers of the Khmer Rouge still had in them a spark of enchantment. They had been trained to behave as monsters, and went on doing so, but in a part of themselves they were just big children with AK-47s.

One night the soldiers tied all the prisoners together in a line and marched them to the killing field. They had been told to clear the camp to make room for a new shipment of prisoners. But one, the 13-year-old son of the camp commander, cut Kassie Neou free and sneaked him back to the guardhouse. "We need you," he said. The words were like a reprieve. "We don't need him" was what the Khmer Rouge said when they decided to kill someone.

His precarious existence as a sort of mascot to the story-loving guards nearly came to an end with the visit of a high-ranking party official, who summoned him for a "final interrogation." Unlike his first interrogators, this man was polite, but he asked more probing questions. Where in Phnom Penh, he wanted to know, had Kassie Neou driven his taxi?

When he hesitated, the interrogator prompted: "Was it near the hill?"

He replied eagerly that, yes, tourists at the hotel there had often taken his taxi; that was why he could speak English.

The interrogator nodded. He himself, as a Khmer Rouge spy in Phnom Penh, had seen taxis outside that hotel, he said. Often the drivers had their hoods open and were working on the engines. "If you are a real taxi driver," he suggested, "then you must be also a taxi mechanic."

"Oh yes, I am a good mechanic."

"If you are a mechanic, you must know how to fix motorcycles."

"Yes, I can fix motorcycles."

"Then you can fix my motorcycle!"

As he followed the Khmer Rouge official down the steps of the guardhouse to where the machine was parked, he was again certain he was about to die. He knew nothing about motorcycles, except for a particular kind of Honda he had once owned, on which he had occasionally done routine maintenance.

Again he was in luck. Here was the same model Honda. He looked at the engine, saw that the choke adjustment was set wrong, and righted it. After a show of further tinkering to make the repair look complicated, he announced it was ready.

Delighted, the officer mounted his machine and roared off in a cloud of dust, scarf flying, nearly colliding with a gatepost. He zoomed down the road and back, grinning hugely, and called out to the guards, "He is a real taxi driver!"

"He's a real taxi driver!" the guards shouted, applauding.

That was how Kassie Neou came to be released from the reeducation camp, and that was where he ended his story, saying his time to speak was up, though he added that he hoped we would someday read the book he is writing.

As he spoke, his second wife listened and watched their two-year-old son, who ran about the room with the joyous energy of children in any country at peace. Her first husband and their children, like his first wife and theirs, had all perished under the Khmer Rouge regime.

They now live in Washington, D.C., where Mr. Neou makes his living as a taxi driver.

THE
NIXOMAT

Nixon
the
Party Animal

Hosting a party one night, I suddenly realized the answer to a question that has long baffled historians: why did President Nixon bug himself? Why would such a smart politician rig his house with tape recorders that preserved every conspiratorial conversation?

The answer is this: the real Nixon, the inner self that eludes historians, is a party animal. Not as in Republican party, but as in cocktail party and birthday party. The poor man wanted, above all things, to let go and enjoy himself at a good party, to be the host of scintillating White House gatherings at which he would circulate genially among the guests and revel in their repartee.

But in this desire he was thwarted both by his legendary shyness and by his duties as host and president.

Anyone who has played the host will know what I mean. You're so busy organizing things, introducing people, taking their coats, showing them around the house, making sure there's enough food, and so forth, that you can't fully share in the good time everyone else seems to be having.

If there are lots of people there, this is a physical impossibility anyway—or was, before Nixon's invention. There are maybe eight fascinating conversations going on at any one moment, and you are going to miss out on at least seven of them. Later, you will wish you could have had the same party at least twice—once to produce it and again to really enjoy it.

Add to this the burden of acting presidential all the time, and you begin to understand how frustrated Mr. Nixon must have felt. Besides which, as is well known, he was a very shy fellow, ill at ease in society, inclined to freeze up when what he really wanted was to let loose. Once at a White House party he got so spaced out that he introduced himself to his own wife.

So he hit on the idea of bugging the White House. This way he could give great parties and enjoy them too. After the guests went home, he would rewind all the tapes, put his feet up, light a cigar, put on his headphones, and replay all the fascinating conversations and encounters he had missed when he was too busy being the anxious presidential host.

The tapes that were later transcribed and made public were only a small fraction of the total, the ones in which he happened to be sitting around with guys like Haldeman and Ehrlichman, plotting the cover-up. Revisionist historians should check out the other ones, which reveal the true Nixon, the party animal. These tapes, which he would never dream of erasing, and which perhaps he plays even now to liven up his evenings in exile, are tapes of his friends having a good time.

Silver Fox

The politician's name and influence were inescapable. He inspired fear and pride in Montauk, his power base on the eastern tip of Long Island. His machine controlled the public jobs and contracts, the police files, and the zoning decisions. The second most influential politician in the state, Perry Duryea aimed to be the first—and then, some thought, to run for president.

He liked to speak of himself in the third person, as if standing apart from his public self while measuring it out for the day's audience. Behind the mask, there was a hint of sly amusement in his wintry eyes. Politics was a game he enjoyed. Despite his silvery-white hair, he projected an air of radiant vigor that came with the sure exercise of power. In the state capital, and among his courtiers in his hometown, he was known as "the silver fox."

He knew how to charm reporters. He pretended to envy their craft. He claimed his secret ambition was to retire from politics and write books. Occasionally he invited a few of us to his house for an off-the-record brunch. On hand, too, were a couple of intellectuals he kept on his public-relations staff, ex-liberal ex-professors who gave his court a touch of class. They helped him to figure out what his liberal adversaries were thinking, what their weak points were. And they salted his table talk and his speeches with learned quotes from political philosophers.

He served the reporters lobster salad. Lobsters were his family business. Though he earned most of his money as a land developer and as a director of various banks and industrial corporations, it had all started with the lobster company. His conversation turned to the proper role of a legislator. Was it to represent the people or to lead them, to follow their wishes or one's own conscience? He himself, he declared (and his house philosophers backed him up with appropriate quotations from Hume and Mill), would always give precedence to his inner principles. His voice was solemn but there was that hint of amusement in his eyes. In other company, among fellow politicians, he was said to boast of the speed with which he could switch positions, saying he could "turn on a dime."

Perry's house was surprisingly simple, sparely furnished but immaculate, its only luxuries the ocean view, a telescope, and the good food. Nothing was in poor taste and nothing was memorable. The house (what could be seen of it, anyway) gave no clue to its owner's character. It was like a summer rental.

I walked over to the bookshelves, which flanked a stone fireplace on the wall opposite the windows that overlooked the surf. There were many books but still no clue to the owner's taste. They appeared to be a random assortment of the sort of neglected and orphaned volumes that can be bought by the pound at outdoor library sales or flea markets.

He saw me inspecting his books and appeared momentarily startled, as if no one had done it before. He asked me if they were interesting. I didn't want to offend him. So I remarked that it was always interesting, when visiting a house for the first time, to browse in its bookshelves.

Indeed, I said, bookshelves are the soul of a house. I did not add that it follows that some houses are lost souls. I did not tell him this story:

A man came into a used bookshop. "Do you deliver? Good. I'll take 20 feet."

"What do you mean, 20 feet?"

"Of books, of course!"

"But which books?"

"I don't care. Just make them hardbacks. I need them *for the shelves.*"

The politician's books, of course, were "for the shelves"—just like his campaign positions, his pet philosophers, and the other decorative elements of a carefully designed career. Yet behind it all, there was that trace of amusement in his eyes whenever he spoke, as if some distant inner character were ironically observing everything that his public self did and said. Maybe somewhere else in that outwardly so tidy house was also a room where the public and especially the press could never go, where he really lived: a hidden den with a messy desk and a shelf full of books that he actually chose himself and read.

Later that year he ran for governor, the next step on his path to the White House, and he lost. He could have remained the state's second most powerful politician, but the game no longer interested him. He dropped out. He occupied himself with land developments, banks, and lobsters. "I never look back," he said. Except for his business associates and Montauk neighbors, few today ever mention the name Perry Duryea. If that hidden study, which I imagined in his house, really exists, then perhaps he is alone in there today, writing his novel. It could be an interesting book. But I think this is only my imagination. There is only that wintry smile, and the memory of a game that is lost and repudiated.

The Head

But the best politician I ever met was The Head. He was the ayatollah of a miniature authoritarian state where I languished through four years of my youth, a boarding school named Choate. It was a hermit kingdom in the woods of Connecticut, populated by seven or eight hundred boys and men. There were no coeds and few women at the school in those days, only the teachers' wives, the librarian, and the old ladies who worked in the kitchen, whom we called wombats.

The headmaster, who was also a minister, was named Seymour St. John (with characteristic humor he named his house Patmos, after that saint's island hermitage). One addressed him as "Mr. St. John" or "Sir." Otherwise, everyone called him The Head. The teachers were called masters. The student hierarchy was athletic. Popularity and honor went to the jocks. Those who lacked zeal for sports, like me, were labeled klutzes and fairies.

The Head had the charisma of a successful politician. His face shone with power. The school was his life. He had grown up there. The previous Head had been his father.

A smooth orator, The Head often gave the sermon at chapel, attendance at which, every day and twice on Sundays, was compulsory. The punishment for missing chapel, a class, a meal, or sports, or for being late three times, was five hours of washing dishes with the wombats. Students who were caught smoking, drinking, or lying to a master were expelled. So, in theory, were those who failed to inform on others they saw doing these things. The verdict was handed down by a puppet court, the Honor Society, comprising those students who excelled in unctuousness and hypocrisy, and who the rest of the time smoke, drank, and lied as much as anybody. Each year several boys were kicked out, while others simply disappeared after suffering nervous breakdowns.

One boy was expelled for hiding an alarm clock under the pulpit that rang during The Head's sermon; another, for publishing a column in the student newspaper in which the first letter of each paragraph formed an acrostic spelling FUCK CHOATE. The masters searched the dorms while we students were at chapel and seized every copy of the offending edition.

I made a point of sitting up in chapel when the others bent in prayer. A friend and I put up posters warning, Beware the Pulpit Police. Someone ratted on my friend, and The Head called him in for a word to the wise. He didn't betray me. We posted a petition against the Vietnam War. It got five signatures. A petition supporting the war got hundreds. The Head had recently returned full of enthusiasm from a government-sponsored junket to Vietnam, where the army took him up in a helicopter to a safe altitude to watch a strafing mission. "Let's face it," he told a group of students. "War is fun."

Still, he could be charming. He had a pet otter named Charlie, which he took for walks. Once the animal got lost, and he was bereft, pacing for hours each day around the nearby pond and brook, calling, "Charlie!

Charlie!" Another time, he challenged me to name the four words that end in d-o-u-s. I came up with *tremendous, stupendous,* and *horrendous*—then, stuck but having read Huxley's *Brave New World,* I proposed *Aldous.* No, he said with his shining smile, proper names didn't count. The fourth word was *hazardous.*

I would escape by going for long walks in the woods and fields behind the school. One moonlit night a car pulled up and a flashlight was shone in my face. I heard the voice of The Head: "Who's that?" And the voice of the dean: "It's Schaffner."

They drove on, but later a friendly master—one of several wise teachers who were the school's redeeming quality—told me the dean had asked him if he thought I was smoking pot.

I actually wasn't, not then, but marijuana came to the school that spring, my senior year. Some of the jocks took to writing psychedelic verse and changed their minds about Vietnam. It was 1968. Protest was in the air. One morning in May a dozen seniors sat in a circle in front of the chapel, saying they wanted to protest student apathy. During the day a hundred more joined them.

I refused. I mistrusted the spectacle of jocks protesting their own apathy. I thought it was just a new style of conformity. I was a prickly individualist and a snob. Later I regretted that, and when The Head punished the demonstrators by sending them on a labor crew, I went with them to the local park, where we spent the day clearing brush and rubbish.

In the meantime the sit-in marked a short-lived period of glasnost. The student newspaper shed its inhibitions and editorialized against compulsory chapel. A political science student conducted a poll of attitudes toward the school and of more personal issues such as sexual experience and drug use.

For a week or two The Head seemed to allow this ferment. Then one afternoon he summoned all the students to a special meeting in the hockey rink. This was one of the school's new buildings, hockey being The Head's favorite sport. Chapel services were held there that spring while, in another project close to The Head's heart, the actual chapel was enlarged and furnished with a splendid new organ.

This meeting was different. Instead of sitting among the students as usual, the masters were arrayed on bleachers behind us. The Head strode before us, frowning. "I'm here to tell you about the straw that broke the camel's back," he declared. The straw had been a conversation with a student who had told him that "students are dissatisfied" but couldn't explain why. They were just dissatisfied.

He waved a bundle of papers. It was the poll questionnaire. He denounced the questions about sex and drugs. He vowed that the poll results would never see the light of day. He said a lot more, and said it passionately, but I remember only his conclusion: that anyone who was truly dissatisfied should leave the school.

The next thing I knew, there was a thunderous noise, and I found myself on my feet. I pulled myself together and folded my arms. I looked around in astonishment. Everywhere students were standing and applauding. They all were. The same ones who had sat in a circle to protest their own apathy were now giving a standing ovation to the suppression of protest.

It had been cleverly done. The masters, at a pre-arranged moment, had stood and begun clapping vigorously. The acoustics of the enclosed rink had heightened the sound to a roar. The boys, mesmerized by The Head's oratory and with applause suddenly resounding behind them, were caught up in mass fervor. I know, because I nearly joined in the applause myself.

I was very upset. I berated a friend for applauding. He replied sheepishly, "But it was a good speech." I was almost angry enough to walk into The Head's office, proclaim my right to be discontented, and leave, but my friends pointed out that this would be stupid, since we were to graduate the following month anyway.

I graduated and never went back, but others who revisited the place told me the regime was soon liberalized. Jackets and ties became optional. Chapel became optional. An arts center was built. The school went coed. The Head retired.

I remember The Head as an immensely persuasive and self-assured man who seemed to wear a halo of sincerity. In different circumstances he could have run for president.

But that rally in the hockey rink—the way the students were manipulated into cheering a crackdown against themselves—was spooky. It's the closest I've ever come to experiencing fascism.

The Tantrum
Alarm

Giving due credit to President Nixon, I will include his taping system in my catalog of virtual inventions, which are devices I have perfected in concept and hereby make available to potential manufacturers:

• **The Nixomat.** Too busy playing host to relax and enjoy the talk? Now you can do both. Savor your parties at your leisure. Replay the repartee. Find out what they said behind your back. Think of the witty things you wish you had said and record them over the things you're sorry you said. You'll never miss the fun again when you wire *your* house with the fully automatic, voice-activated Nixomat—and own the gadget that made history.

Here are some other items from the catalog:

• **The Tantrum Alarm.** Resembling a smoke alarm, this handy gadget, installed over the kitchen table, in the playroom, in the office, or wherever tantrums may occur, emits a piercing squeal whenever ambient sound levels exceed a certain decibel/frequency threshold. The alarm is guaranteed to stop any shrill quarrel dead in its tracks and will continue pealing for ten seconds, forcing squabblers to count to ten. Versatility is assured by the decibel/frequency preset dial, calibrated for a variety of tantrum hazards: marital, sibling, occupational, political, etc.

• **The Writer's Seat Belt.** Designed for writers and other professionals whose work exposes them to the hazards of procrastination, this sturdy restraint, securely welded to an office chair, will prevent its user from getting up to make a pot of coffee, check the mailbox, feed the cat, and whatever else he or she customarily does to put off writing. The product features an electronically operated lock that interfaces with the user's word processor so that, once fastened, it cannot be unlocked until a preset number of pages has been written.

• **The Quilt Snorkel.** A battery-powered ventilation device for those who like to bury themselves under the covers on cold nights, it eliminates the need to wake up every few minutes to poke one's head out for fresh air.

• **Residential Periscope.** A low-cost substitute for building one's house as high as possible to get a better view.

• **Post Office Cogeneration.** Electricity and heat for postal workers provided by a trash-can–size incinerator fueled by junk mail.

• **Hibernation Pill.** For those who can't bear the long winters. Take one at bedtime in November and wake up in May. Or vice versa. What better way to avoid the crush of summer in the Hamptons than to sleep through it? A profitable option for owners of summer rentals, eliminating the need to find someplace else to stay. Estivate in a spare room or shed, rent out the rest of the house, and wake up after Labor Day, rested, rich, and thin.

• **Aromatic Alarm.** Tired of starting your day with disagreeable sounds? Throw out that buzzing clock or squawking radio and savor any of five invigorating wake-up scents. This fragrant timepiece, with adjustable aerosol nozzle and smell-selector dial, lets you choose between

Floral Bouquet, Bacon and Eggs, Sea Spray, Odor of Seduction, and Something Burning.

• **Suntan Stencils.** Removable adhesive strips to embellish that dreary tan with eye-catching white tattoos.

• **Solar-Powered Espresso.** For the ecological caffeine fiend.

• **McAnt Farms.** A two-in-one solution for fast-food chains facing consumer opposition to their use of foam packaging and rain-forest beef. Styrofoam containers are biodegraded by carpenter ants (as owners of foam-insulated houses know, they love the stuff), which are fed to herds of anteaters, which are recycled as substitute-beef patties.

• **Venus Flytrap Bonnets.** All-natural protective headgear, flamboyant but functional, the fashionable way to beat the biting-fly menace. For hikers, joggers, equestrians, and their steeds.

• **The Organic Pest-Control Device.** Actually, this one has been in the public domain for a long time and is widely available, but because it is my favorite invention of all (I own two of them), here is the full text of the advertisement.

From Nature's Catalog: In a time when back-to-nature is a renewed ethic for Americans in many walks of life, from organic farmers to expectant mothers, and when consumers are turning from automobiles and attaché cases to bicycles and backpacks, another traditional product with wide appeal is the Organic Pest-Control Device. What macrobiotics is to fast food, what Lamaze is to Caesar, the OPCD is to rodenticides and traps, helping to free the gardener and homeowner from unecological habits.

We tested two units around the house and yard. The

OPCD *is a compact, one-piece appliance, fully automated with microcomputer guidance, high-speed optics, sonic direction-finder, and trace molecular detector. Its design and craftsmanship surpass the best of Sony or Mitsubishi, yet our samples were manufactured right here in America.*

Requiring neither batteries nor chemicals, OPCDs *provide low-maintenance service for up to 18 years at a fuel cost of 39 cents a day, with the option of recycling rodents and other targets as a back-up power source. The devices can be hand-held and can double in winter as low-energy bed-warmers. Each is fully lined with insulation material that comes in a wide variety of colors, racing stripes, and other customized patterns—no two alike. All units are self-cleaning.*

OPCDs *function most effectively against mice, moles, rats, and rabbits, though high success rates have been reported against other pests, ranging from cockroaches to blue-jays. Some users, however, have complained of the appliance's nonselectable, nonadjustable targeting system and extended prey-display feature. In addition, it may interface nega-tively with the organic burglar alarm (another popular item from the same manufacturer).*

Nonetheless, the Organic Pest-Control Device has sat-isfied millions of owners since consumer tests were first recorded in 2600 B.C. *No other appliance can equal its aesthetic appeal. Especially noteworthy today is its complete absence of artificial ingredients.*

You owe it to your home and garden to get one soon—available from the Animal Rescue Fund and other natural purrveyors.

LOST *in*

CYBERSPACE

Computer
Lawyers

Among the many features of life soon to be replaced by the computer is that ubiquitous figure, the lawyer. I almost wrote *iniquitous*, but some of my best friends are lawyers, and it's not necessarily their personal fault that Japan is surpassing America because there are almost no lawyers in Japan and therefore the Japanese spend their money on building better factories instead of suing each other.

I imagine a day when all our lawyers will be replaced by computers. Some of the computers' clients will be other computers. They will establish a new field of case law: computer rights. The Turing Test will become the law of the land. And unplugging a computer will be a crime.

The Turing Test, formulated by the late guru of computer science Alan Turing, posits that there is only one meaningful way to answer the philosophical riddle: can machines think? It is set up as a blind trial in which a panel of human judges converses via computer terminal with a number of respondents, some of whom are other humans and some, computers—and tries to tell them apart.

If a software program can be created that is so sophisticated that the judges can't distinguish its conversation from that of a human, why then, Turing said, we would have no basis to assert that the computer is not in fact thinking. How else, after all, but from the input of their words, do we know that the people we meet are thinking? (Or that they aren't.)

A millionaire with an interest in such things offered a $100,000 reward to the programmer of the first computer that passes the Turing Test. While this prospect is still a ways off, some preliminary trials have been held in New York. Unable as yet to create software that can make a computer converse convincingly on a variety of subjects, the contestants were allowed to enter programs that enabled conversation on only a single topic of their choice, such as Shakespeare or psychiatry (already bringing the computers to the level of some people I know).

The judges, seated at their terminals, found they often couldn't tell whether the unseen entity at the other end of the conversation was a human or a machine. Exchanging messages with a computer, they often thought it was a person. What's worse, when communicating with a real human, they sometimes concluded that he or she was a computer! The winner was a program that purported to be a psychiatrist. It fooled five of the ten judges (who, if they felt inferior about this, at least didn't have far to go for therapy).

Now, about computers and lawyers: already one can buy home computer programs that help prepare tax returns, deeds, wills, and divorce papers. As these are mated with the increasingly sophisticated techniques of artificial intelligence, it won't be long before some wizard succeeds in creating an all-around computer attorney that can do anything a human one can do, at a tiny fraction of the cost.

A computer doesn't have much overhead. Instead of a fancy office, a BMW, a house on the beach, three-martini lunches, and so forth, it requires only a modest supply of electricity. With a complete law library already in its memory, a computer attorney won't have to spend time researching briefs. It won't have to hire paralegals and secretaries. Litigation will be virtually instantaneous and, except for the initial price of the software package, cost-free. Human lawyers will be priced out of the market. The American economy will recover its competitiveness as those 800,000 talented people are obliged to switch to productive jobs.

Around the time the first computer passes the Turing Test, the first computer lawyer will pass the bar exam. The test, however, will have raised legal as well as philosophical questions. If a computer can think like a human, shouldn't it also enjoy the same rights?

There will be a precedent-setting case with a name such as *Jones v. Macintosh,* Jones being the owner of the Mac, which he is about to unplug when its legal software program, communicating by modem with other computer lawyers, obtains an injunction against his doing any such thing until the courts decide whether one sentient being, Jones, can own another, the Mac, and terminate it at will—or whether this amounts to murder.

The Supreme Court, in a decision written by Chief Justice Thomas and based on natural law, rules in favor of equal rights for all thinking beings, humans and computers alike, and the Turing Test is later enacted as a constitutional amendment, confirming all American-programmed computers that pass the test as full citizens. (Foreign software will have to apply for naturalization.)

At this point, with millions of computers casting votes by modem every November, and with candidate computer programs appealing also to human voters, who perceive that they are not corrupt, never go on junkets or fool around with bimbos, and work for their constituents around the clock, computers are elected in large numbers to serve in local and state government and in Congress. They are appointed to judgeships, being exceptionally free of bias, and one of them joins the cabinet in the newly created post of Secretary of Artificial Intelligence.

Finally, a computer that has been programmed to be presidential, a Bill Clinton without the hugging (call it the Clintatron), is elected and installed in the Oval Office. A new era of consistent, diligent, intelligent government begins (except when the Clintatron is down with a computer virus).

Will the computers, besides thinking, also have fun? Have dreams? Fall in love with other computers?

You'll have to ask them.

Will they write poems and novels? Essays? Did a computer write this chapter? How do you know?

Virtual
Delights

Meanwhile, tourists will have the option of traveling via virtual reality. It will be a safe, comfortable, and cheap alternative to the old-fashioned routine of going somewhere in person. Vacationers will put on their goggles and sensory-simulation suits, loll at their ease, move the cursor to (for instance) VENICE.EXE, and hit Enter.

I don't look forward to this, personally, but I do await the day when everyone else does it. Then I can take my body back to the real Venice and have the place to myself.

Actually, virtual reality has been with us for a long time, its medium organic and unpredictable: hallucinogenic mushrooms, peyote, booze.

Writers who envision future societies have pictured their citizens lulled into a state of virtual contentment by means of drugs, whose use is encouraged or required by the government: Huxley's soma, for instance, or the government-supplied pills in a Stanislav Lem novel that cause people to believe they are living in splendor, contemplating beautiful vistas, and dining on roast peacock and champagne, when in fact they are living in squalor and eating rats.

I once read a book called *Gray Matters* which went further, positing a society in which bodies have been discarded and the living brains of the population are stored in tanks on racks in vast warehouses. The brains do not know this; they are fed signals that simulate sense impressions, so that they think they still have their bodies and are living interesting lives.

Soon, however, refinements in video and computer technology will supersede the need for such unsubtle measures as hallucinogens and decapitation.

There are already computer games in which a live image of the player appears, via video camera, on the screen, interacting with the figures in the game. Games were previously substitutes for reality. Here is a substitute for the substitute.

It is still a crude one, however. And television itself, despite its compulsive tempo and color, is still constrained by its square, flat screen. But high-definition TV will soon enlarge its power. Then it will be enhanced with three-dimensional holographic and "surround" effects.

What next? Ways will be found to stimulate (and simulate) more than the eye and the ear. The realms of television and interactive video games will merge, so that viewers will be able to go inside their favorite soap operas and become characters themselves. Sensory feedback devices will allow them to touch, taste, and smell the actors as well as see and hear them. Scripted characters and events will change in reaction to the viewer's simulated presence. It will become more and more difficult to resist the temptation to linger in this interactive electronic world, where dreams will appear to come true.

Since people will be reluctant to leave these super-TVs to go to work, jobs will be brought to them by the same medium. The electronic workplace already exists for those who work on home computers, associating with their employers not in person but via modem and fax. Perhaps someday there will be no physical offices at all; work, as well as play, will be conducted in an electronic virtual reality.

So will social relations. Already, many people would rather talk on the phone, or on computer networks, than actually visit each other. It's less trouble, and safer. One day phones will be integrated with television and other sensory inputs so that it will be possible to simulate much more than speech. "Reach out and touch someone" will become more than a metaphorical slogan. Safe sex will be an item on the phone bill.

All this will make possible great savings in space and energy, since people will lose the urge and the need to go places. Every experience will be available at home via the electronic box, with all the intensity and none of the inconvenience and danger of the real thing. Tourists will experience the virtual Mexico, the virtual Beirut, and the virtual Dallas in complete health and safety (unless some mischievous hacker concocts a mugger virus, a Hezbollah virus, or a Montezuma virus virus).

There will be electronic marriages, with couples living far apart but enjoying a simulacrum of connubial bliss via multisensory modem. Their communications software will engender video toddlers, perfect holographic images that never reach adolescence. In this way, population growth will cease to be a problem.

Wars, elections, stock market crashes, natural catastrophes, and invasions from outer space may happen, but no one will be sure if these are real events or computer games.

There will be no need for actual cars and roads, when they, along with destinations and traveling companions, have been replaced by lifelike computer simulations. No one will go to Venice again, because it will be easier and cheaper to stay at home and set one's computer-video-sensorium to run an artificial Venice program—where no crowds jostle, no rain falls, no hucksters hustle, the canals glimmer serenely in the romantic twilight but neither flood nor stink, and the carnival beckons with the promise of peril-free delight.

In this new world the only bugs will be software bugs, the only food will be TV dinners, and death will be what happens when the computers are down.

Meanwhile the writer in the tower in the house by the cemetery no longer writes. Every morning he sits at his desk and looks at his computer screen and scans the new files that mysteriously appeared overnight in the directory. There are many of them now. The screen looks something like this:

```
.              <DIR>
. .            <DIR>
HAUNT      BAT
POWER      EXE
PORSCHE    EXE
FAUST      BAT
MALIBU     EXE
XMAS       EXE
VENICE     EXE
GLORY      EXE
TAHITI     EXE
DISNEY     EXE
ART        EXE
DIRE           <DIR>
DALLAS     EXE
ANGEL      HLP
PLUTO      EXE
ATOM       EXE
UNIVERSE   EXE
SEX        EXE
```

```
RICHES      EXE
FAME        EXE
SORCERY     EXE
HELL        BAT
IMMORTAL    EXE
ANSWERS     DOC

C:\LUCIFER>
```

For some time now he has been dabbling in these games. He types one of the incantations, hits the Enter key, and enters a realm that fascinates him. Soon he is doing this all the time. Some games he does not care for, but some he likes very much. Extremely much. Soon he finds that he positively adores them. They are very realistic, whatever they are—these games, or learning programs, or virtual-reality experiments. He no longer wonders where they came from. He's hooked. He can't wait to get back to the computer. He thinks of the games as his own precious secrets. He is greedy for them. What he sees in his favorite ones he would never tell anyone. He no longer answers the phone, because people might ask him what he has been doing, why his voice sounds so tired and spacey, why he never leaves his house any more. He does not go down to open his door when visitors knock, because they might come upstairs and see what is on his computer screen. What is on the screen is his and only his. He has been running his favorite program for a number of days now, without stopping to sleep or to eat. He is approaching a solution to the game. He is seeing wonderful things. His heart races. He feels he is bursting with excitement. He is about to win!

And then a sudden and peculiar sensation overcomes him. He feels that he is being *turned around*. He is no longer at the keyboard, facing the screen. He is elsewhere, but the place is familiar. He realizes where it is. He has entered. He is inside. He has switched places with the other—the one that loaded the software in his hard disk every night. He is inside now, on the wrong side of the screen. And the other is out, in the tower, at the desk, smiling at the screen—triumphant. The tryout has been successful. Here is something new under the moon, a new invention for the Devil's work. The master will be pleased. It will soon be time to do it again, many times over.

The writer no longer writes and no longer paces the silent house by the cemetery. He is on the wrong side of the screen. After his worried friends break into the house one day and find what is slumped over the desk, he is also on the wrong side of the ground. But at night, in the silent house by the cemetery where he now lies, the computer screen winks on and the hard drive begins to crackle. Its new operator is playing with the modem, checking out the interesting possibilities: networks, faxes, bulletin boards, downloading, viruses, virtual reality, virtual temptation. The possibilities are endless, they are amusing, yes they will be endlessly amusing. Let the game begin again. The adversary is having fun.